THE
POWER OF
PURPOSE

THE POWER OF PURPOSE

HOW TO CREATE THE LIFE YOU ALWAYS WANTED

LES BROWN

Published 2021 by Gildan Media LLC
aka G&D Media
www.GandDmedia.com

First Edition: 2021

Front cover design by David Rheinhardt of Pyrographx

Interior design by Meghan Day Healey of Story Horse, LLC.

Library of Congress Cataloging-in-Publication Data is available upon request

ISBN: 978-1-7225-0548-6

10   9   8   7   6   5   4   3   2   1

CONTENTS

CHAPTER 1

What is your Life's Work?

"What's going on here? Where is all of this leading?" These are the questions we are all asking. We are experiencing a time of great uncertainty and great change taking place around the world. A time when people are feeling a great deal of anxiety, fear, and reservations about the future. A time when people are going to work and don't know whether or not they will have a job tomorrow—not necessarily because of their performance but because of what's happening in the economy. And a time when there are more challenges than ever before in personal relationships.

Now more than ever, we must begin to look at what we can do to get on a firm footing in life. We must begin to ask ourselves what powers we have. What is our purpose? Many of us go through life never discovering these innate things we have going for us.

Part of knowing your purpose is knowing what your life work is. What is it that gives your life a sense of meaning and purpose? Once you find that, it puts you in your power place. If you do know what your life work is, then I encourage you to start working on it. You don't have to do it all at once, do just a little bit at a time. If you don't know why you are here, if you don't know what it is that you showed up to do, I encourage you to find out what your purpose is here.

What is the meaning of your life? What will be different? Have you ever asked yourself that question? I've done that. I was coming from a funeral, and reflecting on my friend whose life was so promising. I thought about all of the things he had planned and never got a chance to do. I started thinking about my own life and how much time I had left to do the things that I would like to do. At that time, I wasn't sure what my life purpose was, what my life's work was. I thought about it quite a lot and though I had some idea I wasn't convinced. I didn't feel worthy. I didn't believe that I could do this work that I'm doing right now. I had to make a conscious effort to find my life purpose. I believe that taking the time to ask these questions and find the answers can literally save your life.

Dr. Larry Dossey, author of *Recovering the Soul*, reports that human beings are the only species that have achieved the dubious distinction of dying on a certain date. In this country, most heart attacks take place on Monday mornings between 8:00 and 9:00 a.m. Most would say the primary cause of heart attack or stroke is smoking, high cholesterol, stress, or obesity. But all of those things are contributing factors.

Now let's consider *why* the majority of people have their first heart attacks on Monday mornings. After the Sunday football game or *60 Minutes*, the anxiety begins to build, and come Monday, they drop dead of a broken heart. According to recent studies eighty-five percent of the American public are going to jobs that they hate, and that do not challenge them. They get sick thinking about going to work. People are literally dying to go to work! If you are going to a job and you already know how far you can go, how much you're going to make, you're in a dead-end position. You can already see that proverbial glass ceiling. It's like going to a movie you've already seen, but starting in the middle. You've seen the end and you sit there all over again. Something is missing. You know what the outcome is going to be. You can't get excited about going through that movie all over again. It erodes your self-esteem. It lowers your sense of yourself. It creates some inner turmoil. It creates a feeling of emptiness.

It is worth finding what it is that you're supposed to do, discovering your purpose. I'm not saying quit your job. I am saying to find your purpose and do just a little bit of it. Just start working at it a little bit. Find out what your work is, hold on to it, and don't let your dream go. When I wanted to become involved in public speaking, I started little by little, going to seminars and workshops, listening to other people's recordings, learning quotes, and asking other people to help me.

Why is it that most people don't pursue their dreams or uncover their potential? I think that many of us don't know what to do yet. We don't even explore the possibility of what to do because subconsciously, we don't believe that we deserve it.

How much time do you spend working on you? How much time do you spend every day working on your dream? In the last ninety days, how many books have you read? In the last year, what new skill or knowledge have you acquired? What kind of investment have you made in you? As you begin to look at where you want to go, you've got to make some conscious effort to begin to work to develop you.

Most people are not living their dreams because of fear. At a recent speaking engagement in Ohio, I met Karen, the young woman who expertly planned and carried out the event. She was talented, organized, and skillful, and we talked about her desire to go into consulting. I asked, "Why aren't you doing it? You have the abilities. You're not here because they like you. You're here because you're doing the job. You're making things happen." She came up with all kinds of ideas but finally said, "I guess I can't see myself doing it. I guess I'm afraid." Fear, limited vision, and lack of self-esteem can keep many of us from going for our dreams.

I went to Denver, Colorado to speak at a major communications company. The person that picked me up at the airport told me the company was planning a major downsizing and had offered some of their employees early retirement and a payout of $300,000. The company said, "This is the last time you can take this offer. If you don't do it now, as part of the downsizing, you might be among those whose jobs get cut and all you will get is your severance pay."

Only fifty percent of the people who were eligible to take the $300,000 took it! Those remaining couldn't see themselves beyond that company. They were afraid to take a chance on themselves. They couldn't see life after that situation. It is the same reason that people stay in relationships where they're abused, unhappy, or unfulfilled. They just can't see themselves beyond that relationship or enjoying life without that person. They think this is all they can do and all they deserve. This is all they've ever known. It's been passed on to them.

They think that this is it for them. I'm here to say "NO!" to that.

"Fear is the most subtle and destructive of all human diseases," said Smiley Blanton, renowned author and colleague of Norman Vincent Peale. Fear kills dreams. Fear kills hope. It puts people in the hospital, and can age you. Fear can paralyze you and hold you back from doing something you know you're capable of doing.

Here is the question I asked myself, and I'm now asking you. What is the benefit? What's the benefit of allowing fear to hold you back? What's the benefit of giving up on yourself, of not stepping out and taking on life? What is the benefit for you? It's one of the things I had to ask myself. I didn't want to make any mistakes. I wanted everybody to like me. I wanted to be perfect the first time I did something. It doesn't work like that. And I had to learn and accept this. You're going to make some mistakes, you're going to hurt some folks' feelings, and you might even make some enemies once you decide to take life on. You've got to ask yourself, "How long am I going to allow this to hold me back?"

Personal development author Zig Ziglar said, "Fear is false evidence appearing real." I like that. Fear is an illusion that we create in our mind. It is a state of mind that can be changed. Let's look at how we can take steps to restructure that fear, to expand our visions of ourselves, and to increase our self-esteem. Webster defines self-esteem as confidence and satisfaction in oneself. Look at your life right now. Whatever you've done up to this point in time, your life is working. Whatever you have produced, it came out of you as a result of the kind of person you have become. It's a result of your choices. It's a result of your consciousness.

Now ask yourself, are you satisfied with what you have produced? Is this what you want? Would you like things to be better than this? Do you believe that you deserve better than this? Are you content? Do you think "this is it," that you don't have to do anything else? Are you already resigned in your life to, "I'm happy enough, I'm not starving or anything?" Are you allowing yourself to get off the hook like that? Do you believe somewhere in the back of your mind, or in your heart that there is some other great work for you? Do you believe that life has something else for you? That's why you're reading this book.

How do we handle this fear factor? How do we increase our self-esteem? You have to begin to fortify yourself. How do we do that? I believe you have to consciously monitor your inner conversation and start talking to yourself, start building yourself up. Sometimes the only good things you will hear about you are the things that you say to yourself.

An audience member once said, "I told myself yesterday for the first time that I'm proud of me. I felt good about that."

Learn to be your own booster. Start to build yourself up. Encourage yourself. Start by saying, "I can do this. I can make this happen." When I started to think about becoming a speaker I said, "Yes, I can do this. I can make this happen." I repeated these words when I was trying to convince myself that I could be a businessman. Even after flopping and failing, after losing thousands of dollars, feeling stupid and dumb, and having people take advantage of me because of what I didn't know, I had to talk to myself because what I was hearing from others was that I was done, finished, and that I had given up.

It's easy to believe what others say about you. Somewhere in the back of my mind I was agreeing, "You're right. Look at how I've messed up." I had to become my own booster, to say, "No, Les. Hey. Come on, man. Get yourself together. You can handle this. You just haven't figured it out yet. It's all right. This is your training period. This is a tuition you have to pay for what you don't know. You can do this. Other people have done it. It doesn't take an Einstein. Get people that can teach you stuff you don't know. Get some people that have done it successfully and learn from them. Take some seminars, attend workshops, read some books on how to manage a business. Change the way you see yourself and begin to take care of the personal details. Understand that nobody's going to handle your business better than you."

Once I started changing that mindset of beating myself up for my mistakes, and started looking at the possibility of doing better—of making adjustments that would enable success—things begin to change. To you I say, stop beating up on yourself. You do it. I know you do it. I've done it. It's a natural inclination for us to put ourselves down. Perhaps we have a negative consciousness because we live in a negative world.

You don't have to teach children to lie. They lie automatically. "Did you wet in your pants?" "No, I did not." "What is that?" "I don't know." You don't have to encourage kids to misbehave. They will do it by themselves. You don't have to encourage them to do the wrong thing. They do it automatically. You have to correct their behavior. And now we have to correct our own behavior, starting with the negative conversations we have with ourselves.

Here is a script you can say to yourself. Say it every day, several times a day. Say it out loud, and say it often.

I can live my dream.
I can find my purpose in life

And I can live my purpose.
I deserve more for myself.
I deserve more from life.

Begin to guard your mind against negative programming. Turn off the television. Don't watch the news. Don't read the newspaper. I think that more people are feeling a sense of hopelessness and anxiety about life, and much of the time you cannot feel good watching or reading the news. You're scared to go to sleep. This negative programming turns our power down and we've got to become conscious of that. Try experimenting with this yourself.

If your job depends upon you knowing certain things from the news, let somebody tell you only those things and start filtering the stuff you allow to come into your mind. Just like the song from *The Wiz* musical, "Don't Nobody Bring Me No Bad News," I tell my staff, "Don't tell me any bad news while I'm on the road. Let me handle it tomorrow." I don't let anybody tell me bad news at night before I go to sleep either. I can't do anything about it then anyway. Why go to sleep with that on my consciousness? All of my staff know this. "Let it wait until tomorrow." And I have a time period. "Tell me bad news between 10:00 a.m. and 12:00 p.m."

After I've prayed, meditated, and read my books, I'm fortified. I'm ready to handle it. I deal with it. Then,

I'm out of there and I'm on to something else. You've got to guard the kinds of things that you put in your mind. If you don't program your mind, your mind will be programmed for you. Human beings are goal-oriented. That's why we're running through life to early graves and why we die early of broken hearts. As Henry David Thoreau stated in *Walden*, "The mass of men lead lives of quiet desperation." I've observed that most of us go through life running scared. This is the time to stop running.

CHAPTER 2

The Power of Positive Thinking

Larry D'Angelo, one of the greatest motivational speakers I've encountered, told this story about his friend.

"Every day when he came home from school, there was a neighborhood dog that would start to bark wildly and chase him. Every single day, at the same block, he would be running scared trying to escape that dog. Finally, he just got tired of the chasing and the running and said, 'Next time I'm going to find a brick and bust that dog in the head.'

"The next day he was walking home, minding his own business, and sure enough, the dog started barking and chasing him. He started running as usual, and then he saw a brick. He stopped, picked it up and turned around. As the dog got closer, he realized it didn't have any teeth. He just put down the brick and said, 'Get out of here,' as the dog whimpered away. All our lives, many of us are running from things that don't have any teeth to do us harm."

Have you ever been afraid to do something and then after you did it, said, "If I had known it was this easy, I would have done it sooner." We create this in our minds, false evidence appearing real. In our minds we make it real. Winston Churchill said, "There's nothing to fear but fear itself." Fear is the destructive monster. Turn off things that can contribute to your fear. Turn a deaf ear to negative people, negative talk, and negative ideas. Start to recondition your mind and retrain your thinking. Start listening to recordings and using meditation on a daily basis. Start attending workshops and seminars.

How does faith come to us? By hearing and hearing and hearing. Listen to things that can empower you, that can enable you to create a new reality and a new life for yourself. People might think you're strange. Most people think it's unusual if you're happy these days. People ask, "How are you doing?" I answer, "Better than good." "Whoa, what's wrong with him?" they say. Try going around with a smile and watch how people react. Most people don't smile, so others may find you peculiar.

Start observing people. Look at their faces in the morning. Here we go, another Monday morning. "How are you doing?" "I haven't had my coffee yet. Don't ask me." These people have not found their purpose in life. That's why they are grumpy, why they're miserable. They are negative because they're hurting and so they want to hurt other people.

Start practicing positive thinking. Keep a journal, record your thoughts, what's happening with you. Keep a journal near you. I keep mine by my bed, so every day when I get up I can write down my thoughts immediately. We get three to four thoughts a year that if we acted on, could change our lives. Don't say, "Well, I'll remember that." Write that thought down. Do it now.

Here's a thought I wrote down today. My friend is in the hospital. It's very difficult. They're talking about amputating his foot. His morale is low. I thought, I'm going to visit, but I can't be there with him all of the time. Why not create a recording just for him, something that helps to boost his morale and raise his hope and confidence? We also suggested he postpone the surgery. "You are depressed. Your energy level is down. Tell them not now. Don't do it now." I know of some doctors who don't perform surgery on patients that are in this state of fear, that don't think they will make it. They have a sense of awareness and want their patients in a different state of mind. I suggested, "What about making recordings for people facing difficult physical challenges? That's a good idea." There are ideas that can come to you out of things that appear to be negative.

My new friend from Chicago is just twenty-three years old. He went financially bankrupt two years ago and ruined his credit. It was devastating. Then, he found a blessing in it. He started to restore his credit. It was difficult, time consuming, and very challenging. He realized that a lot of other people during these particular times also ruined their credit and so he started a credit repair business. Last year, he earned over $100,000 helping people to restore their credit.

A young woman was at her father's funeral putting flowers on his grave. She looked around and noticed the other gravesites were not as well-groomed or attended to. She started a gravesite maintenance business. Out of her personal tragedy, something positive arose. She is now earning more than she had in her previous job and keeping her father's memory alive.

What idea are you sitting on? Write your ideas down. Then, once you get that idea, take the leap. *Take the leap.* A lot of people get ideas and just walk around with them. Have you ever had an idea and then one day, out of the blue you see somebody else had that idea and they had followed through with it? Don't let fear of competition hold you back. *Take the leap.* If you think you could go out there with my recordings-for-hospital idea? Forget it! We'll be out there together. *Take the leap.* It's out there in the universe. If you don't take the plunge, I guarantee you somebody else will. Take the plunge. Go into action. You will be surprised how things will come together.

I have to tell you this now: You are going to have some difficult challenges. Things are not going to work out exactly right. For a time, they might. But there are many times when life will just come over and slap you on the side of the head. I'm telling you this now so you will not become undone if this happens.

Go into action with your dream. Don't avoid things because there might be a fight. Get in the midst of it; get knocked down so you can learn to hold your position. Most people don't get out in the arena of life because they don't want to fight or get knocked down. But you're going to be knocked down whether you're on the field or you're sitting on the sidelines. So at least get dropped for something. Don't get knocked down while you're sitting down. Most people are spectators in life. You don't want to be a spectator. You want to get out in the field where the action is. You will be amazed, after the struggle there will be a calm period, and then things will begin to click for you.

You don't have enough money? Don't worry about it. You have the idea. You have the dream. You don't have enough resources? Don't worry about it. You need some help? Don't worry about it. Get out there in the arena. Someone will look at you, become inspired and say, "Hey, can I help you?" If you are sitting up on the bleachers, nobody's going to ask you anything. You've got to get out into the action.

I got a call from Frances Hart in Chicago. For ten years she had been sitting on an idea for a show she wanted to produce called *Mind-Body Connection*. Someone she knew saw me speaking at a convention in Chicago and told her "Perhaps Les Brown can help you host this show. He has the energy and charisma." So she called me. She was so fired up. I said, "Listen, I'm speaking in Chicago that day and I can do it for you. By the way, I met someone in Baltimore two weeks ago with a similar idea and she's doing it on radio. Why don't you call her?"

She did and then she called back. "Who else would you suggest?" she asked. "Well, I know Deepak Chopra who wrote the book *Quantum Healing* and I know Bernie Siegel." I put her in touch with another friend who could get her in touch with them. She started calling all around, just as she had called me on a suggestion. Frances did not have the resources, only this idea and this dream. When we finally came together in the studio before the audience she said, "I feel like I've been pregnant for ten years and tonight you are going to witness a beautiful delivery." And it was. She said, "Les, I can't believe how things began to happen, and once it started, how it all began to come together so quickly."

You don't have to have all your stuff together. Sometimes, if you just go out there with your dreams and your faith, things can begin to happen for you. You won't know until you give it a try. Go ahead. Take a chance. You can do it.

CHAPTER 3

The Power of Hard Times

Experience the pain. Experience the rejection. Experience the hard times. That's how you grow. That's how you develop yourself. That's how you begin to appreciate the things you get. When you're working toward your dream, at some point a transition takes place. The transition is what you're becoming as you pursue your dream. And even if you don't achieve that dream, you become such a strong and powerful person just in the striving toward it. It will change your life and outlook in powerful ways. Now you can look at something else and say, "Well then, I think I'll go do this."

As you strive to pursue your dream, you are developing competence and confidence in yourself. You are learning how to deal in the arena of life and you can move into another area and not miss a beat. Once you begin to discover who you are, you realize how you have been given authority and dominion over everything on the face of the earth, especially all the dimensions of your own life. However, you can only do that by going through the struggles of life.

Most people avoid the struggle and go through life avoiding pain. When you go through life like this, something in you dies. There is something lying dormant in you, something that you never activate because you have not challenged yourself. It is said, "The land of familiarity belongs to the dead." People like to feel comfortable. They like being the king of their comfort zone and only do those things they know how to do well. Unless you attempt to do something beyond that which you've already mastered, you will never grow.

To begin to grow, you've got to put something out there that you can't reach easily, a goal that will make you stretch, make you jump for it, something to make you get back a little and dig in, so that you can take a leap forward. Maybe you jump up there and you miss it, you skin your knees. Then you come back again and you bust your lip, but you keep on, and through that process, you learn how to leap higher. You start challenging yourself to dig deeper.

You will discover some things about yourself that you didn't know; talents and abilities you didn't know you had. I started out just talking to kids. Now I'm speaking at corporations, traveling, and motivating large audiences everywhere. Had I not pushed for it I wouldn't have known this was something I could do. I had to give myself the chance to try. Give yourself a chance. And here's something else that is very important. If you want to make your stuff happen, it is crucial that you start trusting yourself. Listen to yourself. Listen to that small voice within you.

Don't try to make everything logical. There are some things about life that defy logic, some things you just can't explain or know exactly what the outcome is going to be. I think about the Apostle Paul who said you've got to learn how to walk by faith and not by sight. Once you begin to trust yourself, your ideas, and your instincts, life takes on a whole new meaning. You are learning how to walk by faith. Let yourself be led by faith.

Let me tell you about the worst speech I've ever given in my life. I was scheduled to give a talk at Ohio State. For years I'd had a tremendous inferiority complex because I am not college-educated. An associate knew this about me and said, "Let me write this speech for you. You're going to speak at the Ohio State University. The people are very educated there. They're going to notice your grammatical errors, and from the substance of your speech will know that you are not college educated. I care about you. I don't want you to embarrass yourself."

That's how I let her exploit my fear and write the speech for me. I let her negativity about my natural speech be stronger than my positive feelings about what I had to say. I gave my power away. With my permission, I let her influence me into something I didn't really feel comfortable doing. Yet I didn't feel enough inner strength and conviction about my speaking skills to stick to my guns. So I got up there and read her speech straight through. I did not move or take my eyes off the page, as I'm not accustomed to reading my speeches. After I finished, some people gave me a standing ovation. I had read extremely well. I was tense and nervous and avoided the side of the room where my friends Boo and Mike were waiting. The look on their faces said, "What happened to you?"

Instead I went over to the folks that I knew would be complementary, who were saying, "Thank you very much." "You were very good." I wanted to be fortified by this before I faced my friends. When we were finally in the car, Boo, as tactfully as he could, said, "That was *the* worst speech you have ever given." Of course I knew that. "Why did you read the speech? What happened to your spontaneity? You've always been an extemporaneous speaker. Les, why did you do that?" When I admitted my fear of rejection, Boo said, "Les, let them take you as you are."

I gave my power away. Don't do this! Don't give your power away. You don't need anybody else to approve your dream. If people can't see it, it's because it wasn't given to them. It was given to you. Hold it, nourish it, cultivate it, and work on it. It's yours. It's your baby. Work on it until it comes to fruition. I gave away my power until I said, "I'm not going to do that anymore." Now you try. Say it out loud, "I'm not going to do that anymore." Doesn't that feel good? "I'm not going to do that anymore."

CHAPTER 4

The Power of Doing the Right Thing

Always take the high road. Listen to your inner voice and *always take the high road*. Do what you know is right. Treat people like you want to be treated. Don't try to take shortcuts. Don't cheat. Pay your dues upfront. What goes around comes around. You can pay now or you can pay double later.

Sometimes because of our own programming or some negative parts of our consciousness we might have a tendency to say, "I'll just do it this time. It won't matter. Nobody will know."

Do the right thing. Everything matters. I would rather lose out on my dreams doing the right thing than achieve them by taking shortcuts or cheating. I want to be able to look at myself in the mirror. The true quality of a man is what he does when nobody is looking. The saying goes, "judge a man not by what he *says* but by what he *does*."

I believe there's some good out there in the universe that has your name on it. Nobody can take your special good. When you know that whatever you're seeking, it's also seeking you, you won't worry. You don't have to run scared. You can listen to your inner voice and always take the high road. There might be a tendency or a natural inclination to take the low road. You must resist that. Always take the high road. You won't lose your special good. Do the right thing. No matter what.

Here's something else I live by and encourage you to do if you want to make it today. Keep your agreements. Keep the agreements that you make and establish a network of people who will not only keep their agreements, but who you can count on. Create a network that will be there for you when you need them as you'll be there for them.

You might want to set up a test to find out how many flaky people you have in your life. Ask them to meet you someplace, saying, "This is very important for me. Will you be there for me? I need you." Whoever shows up can stay on your list. If they call you, it's okay to be unavailable for them. "Are you busy?" "No. I just choose not to deal with you in this way." It's okay to get rid of all the flaky people in your life.

I once asked a friend of mine about a mutual friend, wondering if they'd talked recently, and she said they had not. When I asked why, her response was clear. "He is so negative. I had to cut him out of my life. I could not risk having him in my life anymore."

I had a fruit basket in my office with plums and apples. I noticed that a plum had spoiled and when I removed it I found the granny apple now had a brown spot. Just like the expression, "One bad apple will spoil the whole bunch," one negative person can spoil your whole life. Leave the flakes alone; people who are seriously not serious. It is said that like attracts like. So if you are surrounded by flakes, that tells you who you are.

CHAPTER 5

The Power of the Three P's—Patience, Persistence, Positivity

I get a lot of calls from people saying, "Hey, man, I read about you and boy, are you lucky." Let me tell you something about luck. There are three important things to have in your life, in working on your dream, and in doing your life work. You must be *patient*, you must be *persistent*, and you must be *positive*. No matter what.

I called John H. Johnson, the founder and publisher of *Ebony* Magazine, for two and a half years to try to get into his magazine. The first time I called, he wouldn't talk to me. Yet I persisted. I kept calling and kept trying to find someone who knew him that could introduce me. I wanted to create an opportunity to speak so that he could hear me. I finally met a fellow who worked for him, and he introduced us.

I offered to do the talk for free, as long as Mr. Johnson would be in the audience. As I spoke, I gave it everything I had. After I finished Mr. Johnson said, "Young man, you're quite impressive. I'm going to have my staff do an article on you."

I said, "Thank you, Mr. Johnson." And I immediately sent information about myself and my work. But the article didn't happen. I waited for a month and it didn't happen. I waited for two months, and it still didn't happen. I started calling every month.

"Hello, how are you? May I speak to Mr. Johnson?"

"I'm sorry, he's not available."

"Tell him Les Brown called and I just want to say thank you very much for the article when he puts it in."

I kept doing that, kept on calling, sending new articles about my talks. I kept updating the information on me and my activities, and kept sending thank you letters. "Thank you, Mr. Johnson."

I was always positive. I could have been negative saying, "Why did you lie to me? Why did you say you're going to do an article about me in *Ebony* and then not do it?" It would have been very easy for me to get an "attitude." But I know it's better to be positive no matter what. When you are negative you're sending out negative energy and blocking your own good.

Don't send out negative energy. Don't take it personally. I didn't care what he thought of me. I knew that I was a nuisance to all of the staff. They get paid to deal with people like me. I wanted to be in that magazine. With a subscription base at the time of 1.7 million, I did not care what the staff thought about me. Any sensible, reasonable, intelligent person knows that if somebody doesn't call you back after two and a half years, they don't want to talk to you. Did I care about that? No. I persisted and the article appeared in 1990.

A lot of people have ideas or dreams they think about and work on for a while, only to give up when they hear "No, don't do that." Work your dream; work on it until it gets hot. Most things don't happen as quickly as we think they should. The Messenger of Misery might drop in on you and say hello. Or Murphy's Law might come by and thump you on the head. Any number of things can happen to interrupt your flow. It's okay. Don't take it personally. Just acknowledge that what's going on is called life, and keep on working on your dream. Continue to keep on knocking, because this is your life. This is what you love. This is your passion. Step back. Don't judge it. As the bible says, "Judge not, lest you be judged." Why? Because when you judge, you invest emotion in it and that emotion is likely to be anger and guess what, anger hurts you. It doesn't hurt anyone else. Anger hurts you.

A doctor I knew once said, "The man who angers me, kills me." Then, he allowed someone to egg him into an argument on the floor of the National Medical Convention where he suffered a massive heart attack. When you're in a state of anger you have so much acid in your blood and noise in your head. Why would you want to take yourself out early by internalizing things? Shakespeare said, "There is nothing either good or bad, but thinking makes it so." Which means nothing is really good or bad in itself; it's what you think about it that makes it bad or good.

The bible also says, "Judge not according to appearances, but right judgment," which guides us to look beneath the surface and judge correctly. Focus forward. Focus on your dreams and feel that everything is going to work out because you're patient, you're persistent, and you're going to be positive, no matter what. Don't allow other things, people, or circumstances to determine what your reaction is going to be.

I was out to dinner with some people and we had a waitress that was quite discourteous and rude. The people around me took an attitude about it. It was uncomfortable, and emotions were heating up. I've learned how to observe life. I think that in order to overcome friction, you've got to learn how to observe and just stand back, watch what's going on and choose not to buy into it, and choose responses carefully.

I said to her, "Excuse me, ma'am. Do you know what tip stands for?" She said no. I said, "TIP stands for To Ensure Promptness. We've been sitting here a long time. I want to give you $20 upfront to ensure a prompt meal. Would you assist me?" She gave me the biggest smile and said, "Of course, I will."

"By the way," I said, "I'm not with these people. I'm going to be sitting at another table, so please put my meal over there." I didn't want to anger the person who goes behind closed doors to prepare my food. When I got served I told the others, "Eat at your own risk."

Learn how to observe carefully and watch what people do. Learn to look at it. Don't allow other people to determine how you are going to respond to them or circumstances. Learn to look at it and to choose how you respond.

CHAPTER 6

The Power of Perspective

A friend of mine, Tom Perkins, a handsome, articulate man in his mid-fifties, had a tremendous business. And then, at the height of his success, someone was killed in his business and he was sued. He lost everything. He lost his business, his family, his home, everything. He was devastated and started living in his car. He would wash up in a McDonald's across from Howard University on Georgia Avenue in Washington, D.C. He said, "Les, I was so depressed. I had everything and then one day, I lost it all. I didn't want to live anymore." He got some sleeping pills and took them all. Then he lay down, folded his hands across his chest, and went to sleep to die.

Two days later, much to his amazement, he woke up. He thought to himself that he couldn't even get that right. Then he said an incredible thing happened. He was laying there for a moment after he woke and heard a voice say, "It wasn't your life to take." Ever since that day he says, "Whenever I get any major challenges, I don't take it on myself personally. I feel I've got somebody with me. You see, the voice had also said, 'I'll never leave you nor forsake you.' So now I say, Hey, God. You've got to handle this with me. It's too much for me alone. I don't sweat the challenges of life. I don't sweat the small stuff."

This is worth repeating. "Don't sweat the small stuff." Because it's all small stuff. What are you worried about? If someone called you right now and said, "Listen, you only have two days to live," you wouldn't be worried about your bills, or deadlines, or what people were thinking about you. You would put things in perspective.

Here's something else Tom said that I think is important. The voice also told him, "If you change your ways, I'll give you far more than you ever lost."

Look at your life right now. If you want to keep on getting what you're getting, keep on doing what you're doing. You've got to be willing to change your ways. Your life is working, right now. If you don't like what you have produced, that's on you. You are the direc-

tor, you are the star, you wrote this script, you produced this—whatever it is. If it's a hit, you produced
it. If it's a flop, you produced it. Take ownership of it,
decide to go back to the drawing board and rewrite
the script that you are the star of. You have the power
to do that.

On this day, as you read this, you can declare that,
"I'm going to change." As you look back on your life,
you can decide that, "I don't like what I produced here.
I want higher ground. I want to experience more love,
I want to have more adventure in my life. I want some-
thing that gives my life a sense of meaning."

Throughout my career I've had the opportunity to
work with thousands of young people through various programs to deliver positive change in their lives.
One such program was *Project Life* in Chicago, which
focused on training thousands of kids in foundational
life skills and experiences to help them develop into
successful, integrated members of their community.
How life affirming to see these unskilled, unfocused
young people when they come in, become the parents
and the community volunteers when they come out.

We wanted to have a two-pronged program that
would train people in the community as well as those
who are in the jails because I believe if you cage pris-
oners and treat them like animals, when they're back
out on the streets they're going to act like animals, and

then go back to jail like animals. We wanted to take another approach.

A letter I got from a young man in the Cook County Jail gives some perspective. This young man with a violent past—who will not be out of jail for decades—wrote, "Since listening to your recordings, nothing has changed in my situation, but I feel a different person in me."

This gives me hope about the possibility that we are entering an era of consciousness, a time where we can begin to create in folks' minds the idea, the possibility, that we can create a more humane society. With greater awareness of the potential within ourselves, we can create more love, communication, and understanding in relationships. Greater consciousness presents the possibility that we can create a drug-free America, and the possibility that we can create respect for diversity and difference in our multicultural society. And it especially presents the possibility that we can develop the mindset to bring out the best in people, to encourage them to achieve their greatness and support them in their dreams. In this era of consciousness, if we can begin to see and envision that happening, and see that we can all play a role; that we were born for such a time as this, that we showed up for this, that we survived one out of nine million sperms and we have been chosen for this great work, what an exciting time it is to be alive.

Here's something else to recognize wherever you are on the ladder of life. I was reading one of Dr. Norman Vincent Peale's last books, *The Power of Positive Living*—which I think is his greatest work. I was inspired by the section called, "Comeback Power." Wherever you are in life, you've got comeback power. I don't care how low you are. I don't care what you have done. I don't care what you have experienced. I don't care how devastated your life might appear to be, the shambles it might be in. There's a power in you that can enable you to be stronger and better than anything that's out there.

A man came to one of our training sessions. He was a little bit older than our regular attendees. I knew he had a drinking problem. He was looking at me and I could smell alcohol on him. I said, "Excuse me. Come here." He said, "What is it?" I said, "Let me tell you something. I want you to know you've got something in you that is stronger than that poison you're putting in your body. Do you understand me?" He was shocked; he was backing up and said, "No. I don't know, man." I said, "It is there. That's why you're here. Something drew you here and that's what caused you to come. You said you want some help and you need to be around people that can help you get in touch with your power because you know that your life deserves this."

I think the reason we abuse ourselves with drugs and alcohol is that we're trying to numb something in us, something that's aching us, that's urging us, that's nagging us to do something bigger and better.

It can't be because alcohol tastes so good. It can't be because crack feels so good. Cocaine and drugs are not that simple. When we are deluding ourselves or polluting our minds, it numbs us so we don't have to face reality, because we don't know what we've got going for us. Once you discover who you are, the truth of knowing who you are will set you free from ever wanting alcohol, from ever wanting any kind of drug that's going to destroy who you are. Once you begin to know who you are, it will set you free from believing "I can't see myself doing any better."

Once you discover this power, the perfect essence of who you are that's in all of us, that's permeating our being, that enables us to be the directors of our lives, that knows you truly can live a healthy, happy, prosperous life, you will make it in what are called the worst of times. Dr. Robert Schuller said, "Tough times never last but tough people do." You are tough. You are made of some special stuff. There was nobody here before you. You brought something here that was not here before you showed up.

Guess what? Nobody is going to do your work for you. Nobody's going to write your book for you.

Nobody's going to open your boutique. That has been given to you to do. Nobody can help those people you want to help. They will only respond to *your* voice. You will sit here to speak a word that will wake them up as sure as the word was spoken 2000 years ago, "Lazarus, come forth." You will speak that word and ignite and bring to life many who have entombed themselves in fear, mediocrity, a limited vision, and low self-esteem.

Challenge yourself to look within; knowing that you have comeback power, knowing that you came and brought something that was not here before you came. Whatever that dream is, whatever that great work is, don't let anybody take it from you. Fight for it. It's yours, it's no one else's and you can do it.

CHAPTER 7

The Power of Joe vs the Volcano

I like to remember these lyrics by Jerry Reed that say,
"When you're hot, you're hot.
And when you're not, you're not."

It brings to mind the expression, "I'm in hot water." This is something we've all said and we've all experienced. We all have times in our lives when we get into some hot water. Perhaps there's some challenge, some dilemma you've got to handle, something you've got to deal with. Yet sometimes we don't handle them, because we don't want to deal with these things, and then they begin to get kind of hot. Now, we're in hot water. You feel the heat.

When these things are happening it's like being near a volcano that is boiling over and about to explode. What is it that you feel that lets you know you are in the area of a volcano? What is it you feel? Heat. You feel the heat. You're going to experience this volcano because we all have things in our lives that we try to push away and don't handle. And eventually we will feel the heat.

Let's look at the character called Joe, played by Tom Hanks in the movie *Joe Versus the Volcano*. I think there is a lot in this movie that illustrates what we're discussing in this book. I found it very symbolic of my thoughts and ideas.

Joe was going into his job every day. It was a very depressing, dead-end job. He wasn't happy. He was miserable. At this point the movie is very gray and dim, with drab looking people doing the same old thing every day in the same dingy hallway. Many of us can identify with that. Joe knew he was capable of doing more but he had really given up on himself. He had really sold himself out. Some of us have done that. He made a trade-off. For whatever reason, he decided to do this. That's why we can identify with him. The volcano is symbolic of the challenges that we invariably face in life, the problems that many of us avoid handling, and he had to handle this.

How did he come in contact with this volcano? As a hypochondriac, he was going to the doctor constantly.

Because he wasn't living his purpose he would create illnesses for himself. His doctor decided to set him up. When you're not living your dream, you go through life living like a victim and people can set you up for anything. They can run any kind of game on you and you go for it. I had a saying when I was in radio, "Stand up for what you believe in because you can fall for anything."

Joe didn't believe in very much including himself and his dreams. He was very vulnerable. His doctor told him he had a rare disease and only had six months to live; this disease we call a "brain cloud." He believed it. But here's the thing. It changed his life. He was told, "You don't have long to live anyhow. Why don't you do this? I'll give you all my credit cards and this way you can live like a king." But there was a catch. "There's a volcano on an island that's about to erupt. Unless somebody jumps into that volcano, sacrifices their life, the people on this island will perish. Well, your life isn't worth much if you don't have that long anyhow."

"Why don't you take my credit cards, go live like a king and die like a man." Joe said okay. What did he have to lose? He's going to die anyhow. His life didn't have any meaning and value to him as it was. This was no big sacrifice on Joe's behalf. Now that's really something. When you have not structured your life so that it can have some meaning and value for you, you'll be willing to throw your life away into anything.

The volcano could be alcohol. It could be drugs. It could be a job that does not meet who you are, that you go through life just going through the motions. You're doing it for so long; you're acting out that role of mediocrity for so long that you think it's you. It could be a relationship that's no longer giving you what you want and creating dis-ease in your body. It could be any kind of circumstance, like Joe's toxic work environment. It wasn't good for him, but he didn't have the guts to do anything about it. As a result, he couldn't see the beauty of life. In one scene in the movie there is a daisy growing up through the concrete. People were so caught up in the depression and the gloominess of life they couldn't even see the daisy. Somebody might just step on it one day. They couldn't see the beauty in life. That's what can happen to you. You can get so caught up in the misery of it—the pain, the sickness, the depression, playing the victim and blaming everybody and everything—rather than taking responsibility. It will blind you from seeing the stuff out there that's really beautiful.

This is where Joe was. Then the doctor said, "Hey, man, you're going to die with this brain cloud." You know something? Joe decided to live. All of Joe's other illnesses left. Joe decided to live his life. Now, that is interesting.

I heard a psychiatrist give a talk about how his patients reacted when they got information that they were going to die soon. He said that many of these patients had gone through years of therapy and should have been making decisions about their careers, their marriage or their circumstances and somehow, they were stuck. They didn't have the personal power, the wherewithal, or the willpower to act in their own best interest.

When they were told, "Listen, you've got three months to live," or "You've got six months to live," all of a sudden—these people who were initially victims or powerless—they started acting in their own best interests. They start living their lives. What a paradox. Once people are told they're going to die, all of a sudden, they start seeing the daisies in life. They start seeing the beauty.

I remember a monologue from an old movie called *The Last Mile*. A man was sentenced to die in the electric chair for a crime that he did not commit. He was pleading to the jury to understand his case. He was talking to the jury and talking to himself and going through the whole gamut of emotions. The part that struck me and stayed with me was him saying, "It's strange, isn't it, how even though life has done you wrong, somehow you still want to live. You never can find me complaining about life. Life has given me a short deal. No, I just want to live. I'll take the park benches, the crumbs, anything. I just want to live, but they're not going to let me; are they?"

All of a sudden this guy who had never really cared much about his life—now that he knew that his life was going to be taken away for a crime that he did not commit—wanted to live. It was a very passionate, powerful monologue.

What can we do? Where do we begin? Do we have to get a pronouncement that we only have six months to live in order to decide to live, in order to live in a spirit of integrity? Most of us go through life living a lie. The Platters had a popular song that went, "Oh yes, I'm the great pretender." Many of us go through life being great pretenders. We should get an Academy Award for pretending that we're happy, pretending that we're content, pretending that everything's happy, gay, and carried away. That's not the way that it is.

Joe was going through life feeling that he couldn't do anything about his situation. But when he thought he was going to die, he became a new person. He went into work to see the woman he'd been admiring from a distance and finally said, "Hey, I'd like to take you out." He wasn't worried about rejection anymore. He said, "Lord is my shepherd, I see what I want." Joe said, "I might be going, but I am not dead yet." He wanted a little bit more living.

Here's what I think that we can begin to do to live our dreams, to let life take on some new meaning, to give it some new power and some new value—begin to look for the daisies in your life. Right now where you are, regardless of what's happening to you. Regardless of what's going on with your life, begin to look for some beauty in it. Begin to look for some lessons that you can learn from right where you are and what you're going through.

When Joe eventually jumped into the volcano—which he did with the woman he'd fallen in love with—they were thrown out of the volcano and they survived.

Think about that. When you decide to take a leap and you handle your challenges, you are finally facing your fear. Fear is one of the things that keeps us from beginning to live life. John Rodgers wrote, "When people take the courage to journey into the center of their fear, they find nothing. It is only many layers of fear being afraid of itself." Eleanor Roosevelt said, "You'll gain strength, courage, and confidence by every experience in which you really stopped to look fear in the face. You'll be able to say to yourself, 'I've lived through this horror; I can take the next thing that comes along.' You must do the thing you cannot do." That's what the volcano is. It is the thing that we cannot do. Because it is that thing, we must do it. Once fear is acted upon, the death of fear is certain.

What volcanoes do you have in your life? If you had six months to live, what would you do differently with your life? Would you have the same job? Would you be worried about the things that you're worried about right now? Would you have the same relationships? Would you have the same people in your life?

I was sitting on the House floor of the Ohio State Legislature. In my third term, I'd just been elected chairman of the powerful Human Resource Committee, a prestigious position. I was reading a book on how to manage your time and your life. It asked, "What are your long-range goals, two to three years from now? What are your short-range goals, six to twelve months? Then, "If you had three months to live, what would you spend your time doing?" Here's what I wrote down: I would resign from the Legislature. I would go back to Miami and buy my mother a home, something I'd promised myself I was going to do. I'd procrastinated and had all kinds of reasons why I couldn't do it. I wanted to make sure that she was financially secure, that my children would be financially secure. I would do lectures and spend time talking to people and working with kids. That's what I wrote down.

Then I turned the page and it said, "For all you know, you don't have three months to live. You might die today. Whatever you wrote on the last page, you want to spend as much of your time doing that *today*." I looked around at the House Chambers, at the Speaker of the Ohio Legislature. Then I said to my fellow State Rep on my right, "Mike, twenty-five years from now, who would care what legislation we passed?" He said, "Nobody would care one year from now."

Here's what was happening with me. I had come to the Ohio State Legislature with great expectations. There were things I wanted to do. I wanted to make a change in society. I had wanted to make an impact, but after being there for a while, I was just disillusioned. I had introduced some legislation that I had worked months to get passed, got it out of subcommittee, voted to the major committee, and then to the reference committee and finally to the Legislative floor. This legislation was designed to provide protection for senior citizens and poor people who bought money orders. People buy money orders thinking they are like cash, but what they did not know is that there's no bond or insurance security in the event that the money order company files bankruptcy. This company had filed bankruptcy and left a lot of people just holding worthless paper. I wanted to introduce some legislation so that senior citizens would not be victims of this anymore.

After months of hard work and having the votes lined up, a guy raised his hand and said, "Mr. Speaker. I would like to introduce an amendment for Mr. Brown's bill." The Speaker, Mr. Wright, said, "We will hear the amendment." The man proposed a slight change to one word. I said, "Excuse me, Mr. Speaker. May I speak, please?" I continued, "Ladies and gentlemen of the Ohio Legislature, this legislation is not something we wanted to make optional to provide protection for Ohioans and senior citizens. We want to make it mandatory."

Then the guy said, "No, Mr. Speaker, I just think that he's taking it a little too far. This is an honorable gesture on the behalf of the state, but he's taking it too far. Let's make it optional. Leave it up to the goodwill of these money order companies to provide for the protection. Let's have the vote." They had the votes and I lost. I said, "Wait, this is not why I came here." All of a sudden, this job that at one point had so much meaning and so much value, it was no longer there for me.

Many of us have had some experience where you went to a job and you were excited about that job. It had so much promise and then you got there, so much you wanted to do. You thought it was an opportunity for upward mobility, for growth, development, and expansion. All of a sudden after you got there, you found out it was nothing but a glorified cubby hole.

A grave with no dirt on it. It became very depressing going to work.

I used to get headaches starting on Sunday afternoon after the game. I just hated to go to work. Some days I would drive on by, for no reason, just drive on by. I always came back because I had bills. Many of us stay in relationships like that. I had a friend who was so miserable in her marriage. One day she said, "Les, I went home, put the key in the door and I couldn't go in. I was so depressed. I had so much pain in my body. I just couldn't walk in. I dropped to my knees. I had to crawl into the house because I just couldn't. I knew then I had to get a divorce."

What can we do? Here's what we can do. Wherever you are, decide that you're going to focus your time. I lost my job in broadcasting and it was a major blow to me because broadcasting was all that I had. It was all that I knew. I had been doing that for fifteen or twenty years. That was my specialty. But because I was so controversial and couldn't keep my mouth closed, I lost my job. It was a depressing time for me and I could not find a job right away. No one would hire me locally.

I was a seasoned veteran. I had that experience. Sometimes being good can be a liability. Some people may see you as a threat. They want a hire they can control and they don't want somebody who's going to outshine them. Women have dealt with this for years;

having to scale down their ambitions, drive, and abilities in deference to men's egos.

There was a saying when I was kid that an idle mind is the devil's workshop. That's true. If you don't have anything on your mind, your mind can play all kind of tricks on you. When I wasn't busy, sometimes I wanted to call my former boss and say, "Bert, can I get my job back?" My mind was saying, "All you had to do is just keep your mouth shut, now you're unemployed, running your mouth, wak wak wak, wak wak wak. Why don't you just shut up? They told you to shut up, then told you you're going to get fired. No, you had to keep on talking. Oh, ego, ego, ego, ego. Now you're unemployed. Nobody will hire you because your mouth is too big." Stop it, stop beating myself up. Why don't I shut up? Oh, you're right.

So I just kept busy. I started working on flowers. I got really into flowers. I knew my flowers, had names for my flowers, I talked to my flowers. I also did a lot of volunteer work. I'd go to the hospital and read the bible to people. I would visit friends and their parents who were ill or facing a challenge, not to talk to them, but to listen. I became involved in all kinds of community volunteerism. I learned that if you're going through a challenge, the universe is giving you an opportunity to find your real true meaning on the planet. Use that time wisely.

Listen. Volunteer. Be available. Give yourself away. My high school teacher Mr. Williams said something I love. "Love and happiness are like perfume. You can't sprinkle it on others without getting a few drops on yourself." Isn't that beautiful?

Give yourself away. Because what you give, is what you get.

CHAPTER 8

The Power of Change

Sometimes in order to begin to see the daisies in life, you've got to be willing to change—change jobs, change cities, change friends, change relationships. Human beings were designed to achieve. When you're not on a path of growing, developing your greatness, being more productive, and being more effective, your life literally becomes drab, dingy, and depressing.

Yet there is one great human factor that most of us have felt, and that is fear of change. Most people fear change. A lot of people stay in jobs or relationships where they are miserable.

We spoke earlier about the psychiatrist whose patients had been languishing on his couch for months and years, not being able to make decisions. Then when they found out they were dying, they got up and started making all kinds of decisions. They decided to no longer sell out. When I lost my job at the radio station it was as if life was saying, "Les Brown, you know you can do more. Les Brown, you have sold out. Les Brown, go home, go in your drawer, pull out your check stubs and see for how much you have sold your soul."

One of my favorite scenes from *Joe Versus the Volcano* is after the doctor told him he was going to die and he returned to work to confront his boss. He said, "Because I was afraid, too afraid to live my life, I sold it to you for $300 a week. I sold my soul for $300 a week." I know that this is me at different points in my life.

When you look at your life and realize it is not what you want it to be, if you're not living the way that you want to live, if you're not experiencing what you want to experience, you've got to ask yourself, "What have I sold my soul for?" Remember this old song?

> "*You load sixteen tons and what do you get?*
> *Another day older and deeper in debt.*
> *Saint Peter don't you call me 'cause I can't go.*
> *I owe my soul to the company store.*"

This song is a surely a sad lament. And it is depressing to see how many of us have sold our souls for a home in the suburbs or a brand new car or popularity.

When you decide to make a change, it's challenging. There is going to be some resistance. Not everybody will agree with you. There's a price to pay.

Sometimes you stay in a situation too long. Many times, you say, "Well, I need to do it for the kids." Actually, staying too long can be harmful to the kids. A friend of mine who finally got a divorce after years of agonizing told me, "I stayed there as long as I did for the kids, but if I had to do over again, I would have left sooner because it wasn't healthy for them, and it wasn't healthy for me." Many of us stay in jobs where it's no longer good for us to be there. We can't see ourselves having the capacity to do more, to achieve more, and we can't see life after that job, so we stay there as victims. We are volunteer victims, because nobody's making us do it. We volunteer to be victims. We volunteer not to be in charge of our destiny. We volunteer to willingly do it. If you're going to sell out, you don't do it in a hurry, you do it slowly.

I know a fellow who had everything going for him; he went to Harvard, became a lawyer, joined a large, prestigious law firm, married the perfect wife, and had some perfect children. Guess what? He was going through the motions day in and day out, but it wasn't giving him what he wanted out of life. He was doing an act, playing a role. One day he couldn't get out of bed. He couldn't get up, he was paralyzed. Doctors looked at him, examined him from head to toe, and said there's nothing physically wrong with him. "Get up, John. Come on, get up." But he couldn't get up. He stayed like that for months because there was conflict in his body, there was dis-ease.

Many times, when life is calling on us to change and to grow and to expand we say, "No, I don't want to hear that. No, we resist that." We can go back to that lifestyle of mediocrity. We resist that change, that growth. We go back so we can go back to sleep. Winston Churchill said, "The truth is incontrovertible. Malice may attack it, ignorance may deride it, but at the end there it is."

We know the scriptures say, "You shall know the truth and the truth shall set you free." The truth that will set us free is the truth that we don't want to hear. We don't want to hear it. "You've got to change. You've got to take responsibility for your stuff. You've got to clean up your act. You are not your act. You are there to get your life together." We don't want to hear any of that. We want to talk about the circumstances. We're talking about how bad things are, why we can't do it.

Instead we have to decide to live with integrity in our relationships and the things that give our life some meaning. Stop pretending and decide to become real. Decide that we're not going to make trade-offs because we don't realize what it is we have in our hands.

I'm reminded of the story of explorers in Africa who saw some boys playing with these little rocks. They were playing a game similar to shooting marbles, and their marbles were these shiny little rocks. They gave the boys some candy and when they liked it they agreed to trade their marbles for more. Of course they discovered these shiny rocks were actually large uncut diamonds.

The boys did not have enough awareness to know what they had in their hands, and many of us are like that. Many of us have genius within us. We use it for the company. We put in long hours, sixty or seventy hours a week for the company store. We would break our backs for the company but when it comes to ourselves, when it comes to using our genius on our own behalf, taking a chance with our own creativeness, acting on our own dreams and ideas, somewhere along the line we get paralyzed. We find some reason not to do it.

There are lots of excuses. "I'm not as good as they are. I don't have their education." I felt inferior. I never had a college education so I felt inferior. I thought people with a college education were the most intelligent people in the world. I felt inferior and intimidated so I wouldn't want to speak before people that had more education than I did. Friends would say, "What? Come on, Les, you can do that." "Oh no, I can't," I thought.

"Les, you're a good speaker, man. You can just communicate with people, period." "Well, you know—I'm not—there's some things I just don't know and I just . . . can I pass? Get somebody else. I got a friend and he's got his master's degree. He's real good. Get him, but I just—I'm not the one that comes to speak to that crew." I didn't know what I had in myself. Fortunately, I had somebody around me who saw what I had and was willing to work with me until I could see it, too. This is what we all need, somebody who can look beyond our faults and see our strengths, and hold that vision until we are able to capture that vision ourselves.

How do we handle fears? I was talking with my friend Pat Johnson, the president of *Begin Within* seminars. "Think about some major fear you have," she said, "Take a deep breath, and see yourself strong enough and more than able to handle that fear, whatever it is."

Another friend, Ron Wiener says, "When I'm confronted with a fear, I just practice the art of looking beyond the fear. I go behind it and see it already completed, see it already resolved, and then I carry myself accordingly as if it already is taken care of. That dispels the fear for me." My friend Jack Wilson says, "When I experience fear, I think about when I was in Vietnam, and what I handled back then. I look at what I'm dealing with right now, and the fact that I survived that— the fact that I had other kinds of situations that were close calls or that I was overwhelmed with fear and I came through it—then I'd look at this and say, this is nothing here."

How many of us have had some situation and were overwhelmed with fear? You didn't know how you were going to come out, how you were going to survive, but you did. You survived and you didn't die. Whatever that state of consciousness or that self-confidence, however you stood up within yourself, here's what we know. You survived. You are still here. You didn't die. You are here right now. You got it and you handled that fear. You kicked it out of there.

I'm reminded of a scene from the movie *The Color Purple* when Albert told Celie she couldn't go with Shug. Celie had been longing all her life to live her dream but she was afraid. She felt incompetent. Albert had beaten her down and her self-esteem had eroded. He said, "Where are you going? You can't talk, Shug can talk. You're ugly. You're dumb. Shug got class, you ain't got nothing. Where are you going? You ain't going to make it. You're going to fail." She said, "Look here. I might be ugly. I might be dumb. I might can't talk," she said, "but I'm still here. I'm still here."

As you begin to look at the fears you've faced, remember how you came through those fears, and remember that you are still here. That's a testament about how powerful you are. Whatever the volcano is in your life, know you have the capacity to take on that volcano, the capacity to jump in, and find your true identity.

There's another thing that keeps a lot of people from taking on their volcanoes and jumping into the challenges they're confronted with, and that is the fear of making mistakes, or not feeling good enough. Guess what, you're going to make some mistakes. You're going to make a lot of mistakes. Albert Einstein said, "The person who never made a mistake has never tried anything new." You're going to make some mistakes if you want to do something out there. You're going to fall flat on your face. You're going to be criticized when you come out into the arena called life. You're going to feel awkward and stupid and dumb sometimes. It goes with the territory but it's okay. What's important is that you put your stuff out there. Are you good enough? Prepare yourself. There's no substitute for competency. A positive attitude won't get it. Being enthusiastic won't get it, so you've got to prepare yourself. You've got to develop yourself, you've got to practice, you've got to work, you've got to do your homework, you've got to do your research. A lot of people have a yes-I-can attitude but I-know-I-can't aptitude. Competency builds confidence and confidence feeds into competency. The better you become, the more confident you feel, and the more confident you feel, the better you want to become.

You realize that you have no ceiling, that you can do better than whatever you have done so far. You can go beyond that. Don't become cocky and arrogant feeling that you've already arrived as some people have. That's why they have settled for less than what they rightly deserve in life, because they feel they have arrived, and they say, "Well, I can rest now. I can rest on my laurels. I've made it." No, no, no. As long as you're breathing, you got some more work to do. There's something else for you to achieve.

The publisher of *USA Today* said that unless you've made some major mistakes in life, you haven't started living yet. So if you've never made any major blunders, never made some major mistakes, lost some serious money, or taken some serious risk, then you haven't started living. You don't call not rocking the boat, living. You are going through life quietly tiptoeing safely to an early grave. No, no, no, no. You have got to take some chances. You want to bring some adventure to your life. Say to yourself,

"I will develop myself."

"Sharpen my skills."

"I'm good."

"Better than good."

"Better than most."

"I will keep getting better."

Now say that again, out loud. *I will keep getting better.*

Resistance to making mistakes takes us to the next level, fear of failure. The opposite is just as bad, fear of success. Let's add in fear of the unknown.

I want to tell you about Bob Boyd from Columbus, Ohio, who I have known since 1972. Bob Boyd introduced me to motivational recordings, to a lot of inspirational speakers and positive thinking, and to a multilevel marketing company called Bestline Products. I've been involved in business deals with him. I had not seen Bob for a number of years, and when he wanted to come and see me I was interested. Here's why. Bob has incredibly had at least thirty failures since I've known him. I wanted to know if Bob had lost his fire, if life had beaten his dream out of him.

"Hello Les, I've got to talk to you." He greeted me in the traditional Bob Boyd fashion, "Les Brown, I've got a deal I know can expose you to a lot of people. Man, I've got a deal." I'm thinking, "Does he want me to join Amway? What is this?"

"Man, I've got something going. Man, this thing. Man, Les, it's a money machine."

I said, "Tell me about it, Bob," but here's what was going on in my mind. Bob didn't mention anything at all about the deals he'd lost money on. It never came up in conversation. It was like this is the first deal he ever brought me. "What courage," I thought.

I like what Winston Churchill said about courage. "Courage is the ability to go from failure to failure without losing enthusiasm." Bob could courageously hold on to his dream and not lose enthusiasm. He has not internalized failure. Things just didn't work out the way he wanted them to work out. He's still looking for his pot of gold at the end of the rainbow.

Bob started talking while he was taking his coat off. "Les, let me tell you something, man. You've got to see this deal. With the things you're doing, you're now on PBS. My God, Les, you'll make a fortune. Man, I just can't wait to tell you about it."

I said, "Tell me, Bob. Tell me." When he got to talking, I said, "Bob, I want to be a part of it."

He said, "Now, explain to me what I just told you."

I said, "I don't know what it is but I want to do it." I didn't even know what I was agreeing to. I felt like Patricia in Joe Versus the Volcano when she fell in love with Joe. Joe decided he was going to jump into the volcano, and she insisted she go with him. He said, "You can't go." She said, "I want to go, too." When you get fired up about something, people will come to see you burn. They want to go too.

I like the fact that Bob has not lost his fire. Bob is still hungry. Bob still sees his dream. Bob is still search-ing for a way to make it happen. He doesn't care what people say. That's what you have to do if you want to conquer your volcano.

A man from Los Angeles was on the front pages of all the newspapers. He had finally passed the bar after taking it forty-eight times. That bar was his volcano. He had more than enough reason and excuses not to keep taking it. His son had a law firm. He could have been a legal assistant or a clerk. He was a laughingstock. People joked, 'Taken the bar lately?' 'Know who that guy is? The man making the career of taking the bar.'"

I don't know why people like to see you fail. I was on the expressway and traffic was jammed up. You know what was happening? There was an accident and people pulled over to the side to get out of their car to go look; to see somebody else's suffering. That's why talk shows are so popular. People get caught up in other people's misery, and then they go magnify it in their own lives. That's all they focus on.

Bob Boyd went to conquer his volcano just like that Los Angeles gentleman did. He decided it didn't matter how many times he failed. He was going to courageously pursue the bar exam. He didn't care what people said. He didn't care what people think. This was something that he wanted to do to give his life meaning and value. You've got a volcano like that in you somewhere. At some point in time, all of us have seen our destiny.

Reverend Ed Graham of Mt. Zion Baptist Church in Miami came to visit when I was six years old. It was right before Christmas, and my mother was ill. We had no food in the house, and this tall strapping man came to the door with a food basket in his hand, and said, "Hello? Is this the Brown family?" My mother said, "Yes." He continued, "I understand you have two sons and a daughter and that you have no food. I'm from Mt. Zion Baptist Church and around Christmastime, we pass out food baskets to needy families. Please take the basket on behalf of the church and have a nice Christmas." When he walked out, I said, "Oh boy, I'd like to be like that man." I went to his church and I watched him speak—he was a powerful and dynamic speaker with such eloquence. One of his favorite people was the poet Rudyard Kipling who wrote, *"If you can keep your head when all about you are losing theirs and blaming it on you."*

My high school friend, and former fiancée, Mildred Singleton once observed eye surgery from a distance during a school outing to a hospital. She said, "That's what I want to do." She was just a teenager then and today she's an ophthalmologist. All of us have seen our destiny at some point in time. Maybe we decided to ignore it, and said, "No, that's not for me. Life came in and stuff decided to hit, and we stopped dreaming anymore."

Bigger Thomas, the main character in Richard Wright's novel, *Native Son* said, "The impulse to dream has been slowly beaten out of me through the experience of life." That's what causes many of us to give up on our volcano. The experiences, challenges, defeats, disappointments, and the failures of life are sometimes so overwhelming that we decide to prematurely throw in the towel on ourselves—to sell out on our true potential, and on living our dreams. You don't want to make any mistakes, especially if you were raised with a great deal of criticism. You've got to be willing to prepare yourself and do the best you can. Take your best shot and let the chips fall where they may.

People become afraid of success because they feel they're not good enough, that they won't be able to handle it. That the responsibility is too big. I've been there, and when you feel that way, you begin to unconsciously work against yourself to make sure that you don't get it. You begin to sabotage your own potential in a variety of ways—through procrastinating, not giving reports on time, not spending your time wisely—either by looking at a lot of idle television or spending all your time lamenting and complaining about how bad things are—by using your energy negatively rather than positively, or by complaining rather than producing. That's what we do when we're afraid of really making it. When you're afraid of the unknown, when you're afraid to take that leap, when you're afraid to venture out there, overcoming that fear is the real challenge.

A little boy and his friend were out playing on some ice that was supposed to have been solid, but one stepped on a thin area of the ice and fell in. He started thrashing in the water, moving with the undercurrent to other areas underneath the ice. His friend was trying to help him, beating and hitting the ice, trying to save him. He noticed a tree just a short distance away. He ripped off a branch and started scraping around the ice to make a circle. Then he started pounding on it and beating on it. All of sudden the ice crumbled and he was able to pull his friend out to safety. When the paramedics finally got there, they saw what had happened. He had saved the little boy's life. What baffled the paramedics was *how* he did it. They looked at the big branch, and the thickness of the ice, and finally at this little, scrawny boy and said, "How did he do this? It's impossible." They just went beating around the ice to see how thick it was, hearing the thumping sound. It was a miracle that he was able to just take that branch and go around, make a circle, and beat the ice and pull him through just two small gaps—it's just seemed impossible. An old man standing nearby heard the conversation. He stepped forward and said, "I can tell you how he did it. He didn't have anybody here to tell him he couldn't do it."

Sometimes life will happen to you like it did for this little boy and you won't have time to say no. You won't have time to think that you can't do it. The only time you will have is to act, to take the leap of faith, and believe that everything is going to be all right. Take that leap of faith. Trust yourself, and know within yourself that every thing's going to be all right.

The only guarantee in life is this: you are going to die. In case you didn't understand that let me put it another way; you can't get out of life alive. I'm saying to you now, you have six months left to live. Live your life *now*. Live your dreams *now*. Start acting like this is your last day on the planet. We need to decide that we don't need a pronouncement from some physician giving us only six months to live in order to really begin to appreciate the beauty of life. In order to really make some hard decisions in life. We have the power in our hands. Like those little boys, we have that kind of power, that kind of genius, that kind of fortune, that kind of wealth, that kind of happiness, that kind of sense of fulfillment, in our hands *right now*. It's on us and nobody can make the decision for us. We can go through life and resign ourselves to be miserable as we go to our graves, looking good for everybody else except to ourselves, or we can decide,

"Hey, wait. This is the only life that I have, and that is my volcano."

I'm going to take the leap of faith. I'm going to jump in it and I'm going to handle it because I know the universe will never give me anything I don't have the capacity to handle. You've got the power within you to handle any kind of volcano in your life regardless of how it shows up, regardless of any kind of challenge that you might have in your life. You have got that in you right now. Where will it come from? If you trust yourself, it will come to you just when you need it. I believe there's something about life, that when a person resolves within themselves that this is how I give my life, this is how I'm forwarding myself in the universe, then the universe will support you.

Dr. Johnny Youngblood, of New York, said to me, "I must live what's in me. This is why I've got to do this, Les. I must live what's in me, and all of us have something in us that we must live." If we don't know what it is right now, we must create it or we must find it. All of us have this whatever this something is that gives our life that meaning, that value, that power, and that happiness. Pay no attention to those people who just can't understand why you've got to take on that mountain. They won't understand you. Don't you know there are people who've decided that what they are doing is who they are? They've been acting this way for so long, they think their act is who they are. They've been evading themselves so long that mediocrity is natural to them. They won't understand why you've got to go and do what you've got to do, why you might have to change cities or get a different job. They will say, "Why? This job is paying well."

"It's not the pay. It's not always the money. Yes, I need money but I need something else other than money. I need some peace of mind. I need some fulfillment within me. It's not giving me what I want."

"What is it?"

"I don't know."

"Why do you have to go? Why are you going now?"

"I just—I don't want to live this way anymore."

"Why?"

"I don't expect you to understand."

He who knows, needs no explanation, and he who does not know, no explanation will suffice. "I just got to go and jump in the volcano. Excuse me."

Design your life so that it makes sense to you. It might not make sense to anybody else but it makes sense to you. That's what's important. It makes you happy. It gives you that sense of joy. It brings back alive that little boy or little girl in you. This is Mrs. Mamie Brown's little boy, Leslie Calvin Brown saying, "Go get your volcano!

CHAPTER 9

The Power of Purpose

In this chapter I want to talk about *critical options*. Some words we can use to define critical options would be: decisions, choices, preferences, desires, and self-determination. In life, you have critical options. You can take a stand in your life or you can follow the crowd. People who follow the crowd are not living lives that are focused. They're not immersed in anything. People who will take a stand are living a life that has some power, a life of achievement, a life that has some meaning. People who are taking a stand in life are consciously involved in a process to design a life of substance. People who are following the crowd are just doing what everybody else is doing. They're following the followers. I want you to think about this critical question. What is the focus of your life?

What are some of the things we can do that will enable us to live our lives with purpose and meaning? How can we live in a way that can be real for us, that can give us a sense of fulfillment, of joy and happiness, and peace of mind? Many people are bored with life. Many feel that life isn't worth the hassle, that life is just wearing them out. It's boring. They have nothing to look forward to. It's monotonous. Here we go again, another Monday morning. TGIF, thank God it's Friday. So let us not be followers. Let us not walk around with a bored and weary face and let's look at some of the ways we can begin to give our lives some special power.

The first thing you can do is to commit yourself to giving your best at all times. That's not easy. The world has been changing fast and people are realizing they've got to change their behavior. We are now involved in a world economy and that means we cannot do business the same way as in the past. The standards have been raised. We will never be able to do just enough to get by. Quality and productivity have been increased because of the competition, and average performance will not be enough. This is a new day. Competition is fierce, so people who are locked into behavior patterns of just working hard enough to keep from getting fired are being laid off or forced into early retirement.

It's a new game. It's about increased productivity and about superior quality service. Now more than ever, it's about creating a positive atmosphere in the workplace. People are focused and competitive, and hungry to make it. So you need to be hungry, to show you have drive. You can't just casually walk around, "Well, I'll get to it later on." Oh no, no. This is a new day right now. Commit yourself to giving your best at all times. Pay no attention to careless or lazy influences that carelessly tell you, "Hey, look. Don't push yourself too much." Now is the perfect time to push yourself, to get in the habit of giving the best that you have to share.

I'm going to share from my own life a perfect example of giving the best at all times. I was giving a lecture out in Los Angeles, California, for Xerox Corporation. As a part my corporate training, I always try to arrange with a community organization to have a group of young people for me to work with in the evening. That night I was to speak at Carson Community Center right outside of Los Angeles. I had met with one of the young organizers and his mother. This young man took an interest in me because we were both twins.

Sadly his brother had been the victim of a gang initiation ritual, killed as he was coming out of a store by a new member proving their loyalty to the gang with a random killing. They were very interested in having me speak. "Mr. Brown, would you please come and talk to the teenagers here? We are very interested in your workshops and your materials and handouts. There's a lot of depression and despair and hopelessness here, and people are feeling powerless about the gangs. Parents will be involved too. Would you be willing to do that?" I said, "Well, I'm doing a full-day seminar and I'm usually just physically exhausted afterwards. How many people are you going to have?" "We guarantee at least 400 to 500 people there." I said, "Okay. I will come there and work with them and take them through this intense workshop called Project Respect. We will look at how to create a shift in the community, how to get young people engaged in the process of creating positive peer pressure. I'll give instruments and techniques for how we can provide ongoing coaching for young people to begin to change how they see themselves and their values, and how to resist negative peer pressure."

I came there after working the seminar all day, totally exhausted. In that Los Angeles traffic, it took over an hour to get there. When I finally got there, they only had seven people. I had an attitude. I said, "You had me come all the way from Los Angeles? After working all day? Just to talk to seven people? You told me over 400 people were going to be here? Where are the parents? There's only one parent here. My time is valuable. I've got all this material I copied to do a workshop!"

So I talked to those seven young people. I just gave them a little speech, and then I left. That night, around 3:30 AM, the phone rang at my hotel. It was the minister that had arranged the workshop saying, "Mr. Brown, I've got to ask for your attention for a moment. Kenyatta, one of the young men who was there tonight, wants to talk to you. It was his twin brother that was killed. He's been here for over an hour and I asked him not to call you but he insisted. Would you please talk to him for a moment?" I said, "Yes. Put him on the phone. Kenyatta, what can I do for you?"

He said, "Mr. Brown, I listened to your recordings for a long time. I've grown to love you and admire you. Among the things that I heard on your recordings was that you said you must deal with circumstances such as you find them. You came in this evening and I admit, no, we did not have the numbers that you asked for. No, we did not deliver as we had promised we would, but we were looking for you, the motivator, to give us some hope. We are depressed and we don't know what to do. We were looking for some direction and you were so caught up and pouting with your ego because we didn't have the place full. You didn't give us your best."

I sat up in the bed. I said, "Excuse me. Wait a minute here. I worked all day. I didn't charge you a quarter for any of this. I spent time copying materials and traveled there after my full day. I was there to give a training workshop and all you had to do was bring people there. If you don't do it for me, at least provide the next speaker an audience for him to work with."

One thing I have learned is that it is hard to get feedback and even constructive criticism can be hard to hear. We become defensive and we start to justify. So I took his remarks personally.

Kenyatta listened to my rant and then asked, "Are you through, sir?"

I said, "Yes."

He continued, "Mr. Brown, you said you must deal with circumstances such as you find them." We went round and round for about 45 minutes because my ego was on the line. I couldn't let this young man out-debate me. He was not intimidated. I used all the verbal gymnastics and examples I could think of. He would not budge and finally I said, "Okay, I'm sorry. Give me a break, please." He said, "It takes a big man to say he's sorry."

After we hung up from the call, I stood by the bed and prayed. "Lord if you ever give me a chance to speak again, I don't care if it's only one person in the audience. I'm going to wear that one out."

I learned my lesson. When you start looking at what it takes to commit to giving your best at all times, it's clearly not easy, yet those are the standards you are setting for yourself because that's who you are. Let's say you're working on a job where you're miserable, they're not paying you what you're worth. You don't like the work, you don't like the people, and you're dissatisfied. If you decided to continue to take a paycheck, you owe it to yourself to give it your best effort. If you get in the habit of being mediocre or doing just enough to get by, you're not hurting anybody but yourself. You're cheating you.

I want to share the following story that touched me very much. It is a modern parable that gets right to the heart of doing your best at all times.

The Builder

There was a man who was a skilled and efficient builder. He had worked for years in a large company and had reached the age of retirement. His employer asked him to build one more house. It was to be his last commission. The builder took the job but his heart was not involved. He used inferior materials. Timber was poor and he failed to see the many things that should have been clear to him had he shown even his normal interest in his work. When the house was eventually finished, his employer came to him and said, "The house is yours. Here's the key. It's a present from me." The builder immediately

regretted that he had not used the best materials and engaged the most capable workers. If
only he had known that the house was for him.

This story really moves me. If only he had made a
commitment with his life, with his craft, saying, "I'm
going to give my best at all time, even if this is my
last job, I'm going to give it my best shot because that
expresses who I am," he would have had the gift of his
lifetime.

The next critical option that will enable us to live our
lives with purpose and meaning is to decide to live
each day with integrity. Don't try to get something over
in life. Don't try and cheat. Cheating is so easy. I was
at a service station with a friend getting some gas and
they gave me too much change. I discovered it down
the road and was turning around to go back. My companion said, "You fool. Do you think they flag people
down when they don't give the right change?" I said,
"I'm not responsible for them. I'm responsible for me."

I went back and said, "Excuse me, sir. You gave me a
$20 bill too much." He just took it and walked away, no
"Thank you." My companion said, "I told you, you fool.
I'd have kept it." I said, "I'm not responsible for his attitude. I would still give it back to him even knowing he
would not say thank you because my image of myself

says you don't take something that doesn't belong to you. That's the way my mother raised me." Don't try and cheat. Don't say, "Well, this little bit won't count." Everything counts.

A friend of mine was on welfare after going through a bad experience. Both she and her husband had become seriously ill, and were unable to work and they went on welfare. After they both became physically well, he said, "Look here. We don't ever have to go back to work. We are making more money on welfare than we made when we were working with the Medicaid benefits, food stamps and everything." She said, "No. We do not need to accept the checks anymore." He insisted, "I'm not going to work. You can if you want to." She went down to the Welfare Department and said, "Don't send any more checks to my house." The clerk said, "Excuse me? Now, I've been working here for 25 years. No one has ever come in and said don't send me any more checks. Are you sure you're all right?" "Yes, I am," and she went home and told her husband, "Don't look for any more checks because I told them to cut the checks off. Now, we've got to find something to do." They started a paper route, got over 1,500 customers and were making money hand-over-fist in a spirit of dignity and achievement, not ripping anybody off. That was a critical choice. She could have very easily said, "Well, everybody else is doing it. Why don't I do it?" but she decided not to follow the crowd. I like what writer Terry Cole-Whittaker said, "What you think about me is none of my spiritual business." When you're keeping integrity with yourself, you should expect that it is likely to put you under a lot of pressure.

Another thing to remember about critical options is to not try to cut a bargain with life. Life will not give you any special deals because you maintain a sense of integrity. You've got to do what you do because it's the right thing to do—not because of some ulterior motive that you'll get some kind of benefit or special treatment in the universe. Living with integrity won't protect you from somebody stealing your car while you're trying to do some good somewhere. There won't be any special light around your car. They will take your car too. You've got to do what you do because that expresses who you are and for no other reason. They might not have a banquet to recognize you, or give you a special little plaque and dedicate a day in your name. You do what you do because that's who you are.

The next critical option that will enable us to live our lives with purpose and meaning is to dedicate our lives to something. When you dedicate your life to a cause greater than yourself, you're not following the crowd. I like what Howard Thurman said about dedication. He was a leading theologian and educator and one of the key mentors to leaders in the civil rights movement, including Dr. Martin Luther King. He said, "The quality of life is often determined by that to which the individual is dedicated. If the dedication of the life is vague and diffuse, the qualities have to be poor and weak. There is much to be said for the intensity of life." Most people are not intense about living and can be very casual about life. When you dedicate your life you are not thinking about the odds. Here's a saying we can all live by, "When the dream is big enough, the odds don't matter."

When you dedicate your life, you bring on a special power. There's a power in you that people, circumstances, events—and I'm not talking about the physical you that can change the course of history. I'm talking about the real you; the indestructible, invincible, perfect essence of who you really are that can bring a government to its knees—that can change the course of history. I'm thinking about people like Nelson Mandela, who sacrificed his personal freedom in order to take a stand against apartheid. Imprisoned for twenty-seven years, he ultimately negotiated the end of apartheid and served as the first black President of South Africa. Because of the integrity within himself he was able to dedicate his life to something much greater, breaking the back of apartheid and freeing his people.

Benjamin Disraeli said, "Nothing can resist the will of the people that will stake even their existence on the extent of their purpose for good, that when you dedicate your life to something, you bring on some powers in the universe that works through you to bring about changes that you would never ever know unless you have dedicated yourself."

There is a Mother Teresa in you. There's some work for you to do. There is a Nelson Mandela in you, with that that kind of commitment, that kind of spirit, that kind of personal power, that kind of vision. All of us came here to do something, to make a difference, and in a historical context, the world will never be the same again because you came this way.

Here's something I like to say. When asked how I'm doing, I reply, "I'm doing better than good and better than most, and sometimes even better than that." Let me tell you where I got that from. When I was involved in broadcasting, as a disc jockey in Columbus, Ohio, the first part of my show was an inspirational program. Listeners would call in to the show and we would discuss topics on air. Audrey was one of my regular callers. She worked at University Hospital and was one of those people everybody just liked. Enthusiastic, with a radiant smile, she was just one of those people. Audrey was stricken with muscular sclerosis and eventually became confined to a wheelchair. Because of her physical deterioration, she could no longer care for her children, and had to be cared for in a nursing home. Her nurses would call during my show for her and put the phone to her ear. I would often ask her to say a few words to the listening audience.

One day I got a call from Shirley, another regular caller to the program. On this particular day, I detected that something was wrong from something in her voice. She said, "It's nice talking to you, Les. I'll be seeing you." I said, "Wait, wait. Hold on a minute, Shirley. There's something wrong." She says, "There's nothing wrong." I said, "I know you, Shirley. Come on. What's wrong?"

Shirley had been diagnosed with breast cancer and had been told that her survival chances were not great. During this ordeal her husband became very distant. Overwhelmed by that loss and the struggle she was up against, she had reached a critical point in her life where she just felt, "I'm not the kind of person that can handle suffering and I'd rather just end it quickly." This is the option that she decided to take. I did everything I could to discourage her, to give her a reason to want to go on living. I was trying to find something for her to hold onto to give her a sense of hope, some thread. I used all my resources, scripture and especially the serenity prayer, "Lord, grant me the serenity to accept the things that I cannot change, the courage to change the things that I can, and the wisdom to know the difference."

Shirley didn't budge. I was out of my arsenal trying to hold on to her, to create a shift in her thinking when I asked, "Shirley, could you wait until tomorrow?" There was a long pause before she answered, "Why tomorrow?" I said, "Because I'd like to take you to meet Audrey. You remember Audrey, one of my regular callers?" Shirley agreed. When we met at the nursing home we were silent and solemn because we'd made a pact that she would meet Audrey but that I would respect her decision if this was not enough to discourage her despair and desire to end her life.

I did not know exactly what to expect. I had not seen Audrey for some time. We walked into her room, and there was Audrey, twisted and physically contorted with no voluntary use of her arms. She couldn't get up, move around, or even fan a fly off her face. Her vision and hearing were impaired and her voice was very weak. As we drew closer to her, I said, "Audrey, I'd like you to meet my friend, Shirley. How are you doing, Audrey?" and with what strength she had, her reply was, "Better than good and better than most."

Here is Audrey, who's been a prisoner in her body for seventeen years. She can't turn us off. She can't get up and go to the restroom. She said, "Les, I'd love to be able to get up and walk out of here with you. I'd love to be able to take care of my children, to be a mother to them, to see them graduate from high school." She said, "Les, I can't do that and I'm doing better than good and better than most."

Now all of this had a great impact on Shirley who left there with a renewed commitment to whatever time she had left, realizing she had no right to cut her time short. She had a new determination, a renewed spirit about her.

Audrey could not walk out of the hospital. She did not have the capacity to take care of her children, but she had a freedom of spirit. Audrey was popular with the nursing home staff who visited constantly for inspiration and encouragement. We all have freedom of spirit. Wherever we are, with whatever hand that life has dealt us, we have freedom of spirit. We can go through life whining and weeping, or we can have the kind of spirit that inspires people to say, "It's a blessing to be around that person."

I'm reminded of this story about a young boy on a bus. Some bigger boys were picking on him and they kept thumping him on the head and hiding their hands. He tried over and over to get out of their reach but they just pushed him back down. "Sit down." "I don't want to sit down." Over and over, "I don't want to sit down." "Sit down," until they held him down. He looked at them and said, "You might hold me down but I'm standing up inside myself." Know that there's something about you, something about us. There's a power inside of you that regardless of what happens to you, you can stand up inside of yourself. I think that's what William Ernest Henley meant in the poem *Invictus*,

> *"Out of the night that covers me,*
>   *Black as a pit from pole to pole,*
> *I thank whatever gods there may be*
>   *For my unconquerable soul."*

Remember that you too have an unconquerable soul.

I'd like to share with you something that George Bernard Shaw said that I think has some power for us. He said, "This is the true joy in life." In his play *Man and Superman*, which he subtitled *A Comedy and A Philosophy*, he said that we should establish a tribunal where people would be required to come once a year to give a reason why they should be permitted to go on living for the next year. Can you imagine all the do-nothings? Hopping from one foot to the other, trying to give some justification why they should be allowed to live for the next year?

"Well, what do you do?"

"I drink a little bit."

"What are you contributing to life?"

"I go to work every day."

"No, no. Are you making a difference in the universe? Why should we allow you to continue to occupy the space?"

"Can I come back to that one?"

This is the true joy in life, being used for a purpose recognized by yourself as a mighty one. It's being a force of nature instead of a feverish, selfish, little cloud of ailments and grievances, complaining that the world will not devote itself to making you happy. "I am of the opinion," Shaw goes on to say, "that my life belongs to the whole community, and as long as I live, it is my privilege, my privilege to do for it whatever I can. I want to be thoroughly used up when I die, for the harder I work, the more I live. I rejoice in life for its own sake. Life is no brief candle for me. It is a sort of splendid torch which I've got a hold of for the moment and I want to make it burn as brightly as possible before handing it on to future generations."

CHAPTER 10

The Power of Deciding to Act

All of us, at some time or another, have agonized over making a decision. Many decisions are major decisions that require a certain amount of time, attention and energy and have a big impact on us. There are also a lot of smaller decisions that regularly crop up in our lives that for some reason we'd rather avoid making. They tax our minds, they drain our energy. They create a lot of anxiety, nervousness, and mental torment because we don't take care of them. We choose not to decide, which is a decision itself. Deciding to decide, deciding to act is a major challenge for all of us at different points in our lives.

What are those things that we know we ought to do, that we need to, but for some reason or another, have just not been able to gather the resolve to work on? How can we work through the procrastinating, the putting off, the justifying or the blaming, or whatever reason we just haven't done it? We've all had many experiences in our lives, things that happen to us along the way that prevent us from working through this mental block against action.

You know you want to do this. You really want to do this and you don't know why you haven't done it. This is not easy. In order to reinvent your life, you've got to make a conscious, deliberate, and determined effort to begin. You've got to put all of yourself into it. It's very challenging to act. How many times when you're looking at it, and you say, "I know I need to do this but I don't feel like it. I don't want to do it. I know I need to do it. No, I don't want to do it."

So what do we do? What causes us to behave like this? I think that one of the things that prevents us from acting is the fear of failure. If you've ever failed, you don't want to fail again. The pain of that failure, the disappointment, the fear, can paralyze us. We want other people's approval and we fear loss. Many times when we do those things that we know we need to do, we feel that we might lose somebody that we care about and love very much. We don't want to hurt anybody.

Many of us don't act because we want other people's approval. We want everybody to like us and to accept us, even though that's not possible.

Lack of self-confidence is another reason we don't act. We don't believe enough in ourselves. I have a friend who's been working in a job where she's miserable. She is extremely talented and wants to move on for better work and the kind of money she deserves. Yet she remains stuck, despite having other offers, because of her lack of self-confidence and fear that things might not work out. She won't take a chance on herself. So there she is eight hours a day, five days a week, miserable. She hates to go to work. They're not paying her what she's worth and she knows it. Still, she won't do what she really wants to do, and it's wearing her out.

There are a lot of people whose jobs are making them sick. Check out the absenteeism and the number of people that are depressed. You see them coming to work angry. "Good morning. How're you doing?" "I don't know. Just leave me alone. It's not even 9:00 yet. You're talking about good morning." There are days you go to work; you just want to keep driving past the job. You don't want to stop because it's not in sync with who you are, but you haven't acted.

I have another friend, a brilliant business consultant. He's helped a lot of people start their own businesses. He's exceptionally knowledgeable, but he won't start his own business. He would be able to do it. Everybody believes in him except him. He's so smart that he's talked himself out of it numerous times—the numbers aren't just right, or this, or that. So there are many examples of how lack of self-confidence can prevent us from taking action.

There are many other things that can affect our decision making. There's the old favorite of not wanting to take personal responsibility. We want somebody else to do it, somebody else to take the risk and suffer the failure that we fear.

Many times we pick up our behaviors from people that we love, people that we admire or that we spend time with. We identify with them and we live in the context of their ideas, their opinions, and their life patterns.

We buy into it unconsciously. My mother is a pack rat. She keeps everything. She doesn't throw anything away, and I have also picked up this behavior. My mother never said, "Les, let me show you how to keep everything, and accumulate clutter." I unconsciously picked up that habit. We try to honor the people we love by being like them.

When I had some major decisions to make and I found myself acting like my mother, I realized something about myself. It was very profound for me to see how I had learned to avoid confronting difficult situations and people. My mother has a hard time dealing with confrontation. For example, she is the kind of person who would rather avoid when she has to deal with a problem with one of her other foster children and will call me. "Les, why don't you tell Linda to move? She's lazy. She won't go to work. She runs the street all night, and then she comes home and wants to sleep all day, and I think she's doing drugs." I said, "But mama, why don't you tell Linda that. I bought the house for you. I told you when she wanted to come home, don't let a grown person come there and take care of them. You let her in." "Well, after all, she's my child." "Mama, then you handle that." "But when I tell her to leave, she says, 'Mama, please let me stay.'" "So you say yes and then you call me and complain that she's still there. Why worry me with this?"

Mama hasn't developed the courage to act on that. Some people won't act until there's a crisis situation. Linda started stealing and took Mama's social security check to get some drugs, and Mama finally got the courage to say, "Get out of here and don't ever come back." But she couldn't do it until there was a crisis situation.

Crisis situations usually force us to act, even though we had many chances to act before it grew into such a huge situation. For the past forty years, my friend has been struggling with losing weight. Both of us have been dealing with that challenge. He would say, "Man, I just can't lose weight. I'm big-boned." I said, "I've never seen any fat skeletons. You can do this. You need to act for your health. You can change this. You don't have to go to your grave fat. We're all digging early graves with our teeth. We don't have to do this."

Then, in the last few weeks Bob lost more weight than he's ever lost before, even when we were competing with each other, betting a lot of money as a challenge. He became ill and went into an insulin shock. He didn't know that he was diabetic. The doctor said to him, "You are diabetic. You're going to need insulin shots every day. You have to change your diet. Let me tell you what's going to happen if you don't do what we tell you. Number one, there's a possibility that you will become an amputee. Number two, you can go blind. Three, you can become impotent." Bob said, "Help me."

He became determined. When I asked if he wanted one of my peanut butter and jelly sandwiches, he said no. "Bob, I can't believe you're eating vegetables, man. And you're exercising." He said, "That's right. I'm jogging in place, too." Now he had the ability to do what for decades before had been impossible for him. It took that level of crisis to bring reality into focus and for them to act in their own best interests. Some people have to hit rock bottom in order to rise. Begin to look out on your life and think about what you want for *you*.

As we begin to focus in on what it takes for us to act, we have to talk about circumstances. Things happen and these events can inspire us or force us to act at that particular time.

A friend of mine wanted to do something and just did not have the motivation, the courage, or the confidence within himself. Then his circumstances changed overnight. The company he worked for was acquired and he lost his job. Through the inspiration of desperation he had to act. Life can also bring things that inspire us to act. If we don't have the courage or guts to do what we know we must, life, many times, will move on us and make us act. Life will whoop your butt so bad. You will be so miserable, you will catch so much hell, you'll say, "Yes, I will do it. What do you want me to do? Take me."

A friend of mine said, "I can't stop smoking. I can't stop smoking."

Then the doctor said, "Sam, you have emphysema." Sam never picked up another cigarette.

He said, "Look at those stupid people smoking."

"Sam, you did it for 35 years. How can you talk about people like that?"

"Well, I was different. I'm trying to help them. They don't have to do the same thing I did."

"But be compassionate, Sam." I told him.

Isn't it interesting how quickly we forget? I'm saying you should look for that something in your life. It might be just writing a letter to somebody to say thank you. It might be just to apologize to somebody.

I had a confrontation with a security guard in my office building. He responded to me in what I perceived as a negative way, and we engaged in an argument. I did not like the way I handled that. I avoided going through the front door for a long time because I didn't want to face him. Finally, I decided to act, and I went up to him and said, "I want to apologize to you for the way in which I handled the argument we had the other day. I was wrong. I hope you accept my apology." He said, "I do," and I said, "Thank you very much." I felt relieved.

Now, when you do decide to act, it's not always going to be like that. Once I had a friend of mine do some work for me. The result was below par and I knew he was capable of doing better work. I also knew that he had a fragile ego, so I was trying to think of the most sensitive way I could share this information because I wanted him to do the work over. I was going to pay him for what he did, but I needed my work done right. I was afraid that I would hurt his feelings. I was very meticulous in how I approached him, and said, "Let me share this with you. You know

I care about you and that you're a very talented and gifted person, and you and I both know that what you have given me is not a true reflection of your talents and abilities, and I'm saying let's go back in the studio, and do this again."

He said, "I'm going to forget you ever said that."

He never spoke to me again. I was wiped out. We're no longer friends. I lost sleep over that. I couldn't believe it. I remember sitting up one night, looking at the phone and saying, "I got to call him." "No. I won't." Then, "No, forget that." I called, "Look, man, we've known each other for too long to allow this to come between us." He said, "Don't call me anymore," and hung up. I thought about what I could do to make it up to him. Finally something came to me. "Les, what do you have to prove?" We all want people to like us and here I was acting on that impulse too. When you decide to start acting in your own best interest, you might lose some friends. Not everybody will approve of everything you do. Some won't like you. "Who do you think you are?" "You are arrogant." "What do you think you can do?" "You think you'd get away with that?" "You're selfish."

As we begin to look out on our lives we face some challenging moments like these. It is difficult to start acting in our own best interests. This is not easy all of the time. So what are the things we can start with, to start choosing to act? Number one, you've got to bring it out and look at it. You've got to take the power out of it. You've got to expose it to the truth and the truth is that it has no power over you. Write down something you want to act on, but for some reason you've been holding back. Look at it. The next thing is to ask yourself a question. Is it helping you to continue to put it off? If it's an asset for you to continue to procrastinate, then continue to do that. But if it's a liability for you, if it's causing you some mental and some emotional challenges, or perhaps a financial problem, look at that. Examine that for what it is. Next step, ask yourself, what's blocking you? What's preventing you from acting? Why don't you have the courage to handle that? Why won't you face that? What are you running away from? What kind of avoidance behavior are you engaged in?

The next step is to ask what is the worst thing that can happen when you take action? When I looked at that I said, "What's the worst thing can happen when I tell him this?" He can say, "I don't like you," and he did. What happened next? I experienced that. I looked at that. I saw that and guess what? I didn't die. My feelings were hurt a little bit. I lost some sleep about it, and sometimes, I think about it when I drive past his house, but I'm still here. It's uncomfortable, but it's okay. It doesn't bother me anymore. I've gotten used to it now. So ask yourself what is the worst thing that could happen? Visualize that, experience that, feel the nervousness and the discomfort, and the more you run it in your mind, the less power that it will have to block you from acting.

Finally, ask yourself how will you feel after taking this action? I felt a sense of personal achievement when I faced somebody who had been my mentor for years. And for years, there was something I wanted to tell him, but didn't have the courage to say. Always, I was the student, he was the teacher. I looked up to him, admired him, and held him in high esteem. I was always grateful and thankful for the impact that he had on my life and I loved him so much. I didn't have the courage to say to him, "Please stop drinking so much. You're an alcoholic. You need help." I didn't have the courage because I was afraid that he might not like me anymore. I was afraid he would be hurt and crushed and we would no longer be friends. I didn't want to jeopardize what we had. I loved him a great deal and didn't know how this would affect our relationship. I didn't want him to know that I knew he was an alcoholic. I was a coward. I was spineless.

In the name of love, I was unable to act, unable to try to help somebody I loved from dying. I said, "I love him so much, I just can't tell him this. I don't even know how he would handle it, to know that I know that he's an alcoholic." Finally, after years of this inaction, I developed the courage to face my teacher, my mentor, who had molded me, who's been like a father to me. I said, "I've got to tell you something. You've got a problem. I love you very much. Please stop drinking. You're killing yourself. It's not just social. You do it every day. You need help and whatever I can do to support you in that, I will. Please stop."

I had no idea how he was going to handle this. He just looked at me and I felt something like, "How dare you." We just looked at each other, and then I reached out to embrace him. We had never hugged before—being men, macho men. I hugged him and he just stood there with his arms straight by his sides. He couldn't raise his arms to hug me back. He was shocked. After he got over the initial shock and could bring himself to speak, he said, "I'll be seeing you." He had to maintain his composure because he could never afford to let me, his student, see him vulnerable or admit that I was right. I said, "Yes, sir," and, "Tell your wife I'll be by the house to see you off before I leave." When he walked away I was very depressed at first, thinking, "Maybe it wasn't my place to do this." When you take action, you're going to have some second thoughts. Then I realized, "No. I did what I felt was right. I did it because I feel very strongly about this and I love him to much to stay quiet any longer." Fortunately, he called a few weeks later and left a message, "Leslie Brown, I just want to say thank you," and hung up. That was a good feeling.

When you ask yourself about those things you know you need to handle, what is the way to get started? Write down three strong reasons why you know you must take action. Be explicit and descriptive in your reasons because your reasons have power. Your reasons will drive you when you have doubt. When your faith becomes weak, your reasons will fortify your faith. When you have second thoughts and inner conversations, they will help you stay strong. Your reasons will become your rod and your staff to comfort you, to take you through those challenging moments. So write down your reasons and let them guide you.

When you decide to act, when you decide to take on life on it can be painful. It will be uncomfortable and that's where the growth is. When you're uncomfortable, when you're stretching out, when you're taking life by the collar, you're going to get thrown to the ground again and again and again. But when you have determination and you know that what you're doing is right, it gives you your life. It gives a special meaning and power to you. You will have some power from on high. You will discover some things about yourself that will begin to electrify your personality. When you put yourself in that type of challenging situation you'll begin to discover some things about yourself that you don't know you had.

Here are some words to guide you in this journey. Say them out loud and repeat them often.

I can go into action
On anything in my life.
Nothing is stopping me but me.
No challenge in my life
Has any power over me.

Here's something that Howard Thurman wrote on the decision to act.

"It's a wondrous thing that a decision to act releases energy in the personality. For days on end, a person may drift along without much energy, having no particular sense of direction, and having no will to change. Then something happens to alter the pattern. It may be something very simple and inconsequential in itself, but it stabs awake. It alarms. It disturbs. In a flash, one gets a vivid picture of oneself and it passes. The result is decision. Sharp, definitive decision, and the wake of the decision. Yes, even as a part of the decision itself, energy is released. The act of decision sweeps all before it and the life of the individual may be changed forever."

When you decide to act, to make decisions, you begin to access power within you that will increase your self-esteem and enhance your personal power. It puts you in charge of your life, and life has a whole new meaning for you. There's a sense of personal freedom. It doesn't mean you're not going to have any struggles or any challenges. It doesn't mean you're not going to suffer any defeat. What it does mean is that you're putting yourself in the position to grow. You're putting yourself in line with your higher calling and your highest self and that's what life is all about.

Here is another affirmation to help you decide to act. Recite it out loud, and often.

I'm standing up to life
And the challenges in my life.
I'm going to use all of me,
All of my courage,
My faith,
Determination,
And any help and support that I can give anyone
To realize their greatness.
Together, we can succeed.
I've got what it takes.

CHAPTER 11

The Power of Self-Awareness

One of the first things I want you to do is to take a brave look at your life. Look at your life right now, where it is, and answer these questions. Begin to look out on the future, on this year ahead and take your personal inventory. What has brought you here? Look at the things that took place this past year, did you get what you wanted out of them? Did you reach the goals that you set out to achieve? Are there parts of your life or things that you do that you don't want in your life? Begin to look where you want to go in your life and what you want to do. Are there any people that might be dead weight you could unload? If you have found that a relationship is more toxic than nourishing, more debilitating than empowering, now you've got to make a decision.

Many of us won't be able to move forward because we are not taking true inventory of our lives. Look at your emotional, spiritual and intellectual development and ask yourself how many books did you read? How many seminars did you attend? How many classes did you take to develop yourself professionally, or to improve your craft or your skill? How many new things have you learned?

Learn to take some time for personal reflection. Give yourself the gift of your time—just thinking, being with yourself, examining, beginning to know yourself. What are the things about your past that have influenced you? What's your philosophy of life? What are your beliefs? What things do you feel very strongly about? Are there things that you have picked up along the way, routines or habits you've been doing for so long that you think they're you? Can you re-examine these and perhaps get them out of your life?

There are many things we do unconsciously because we picked them up somewhere along the way. My friend Ria was born in Chicago but had a tremendous southern drawl. When I met her mother, I asked where she got her southern drawl. She said, "My sisters came up from Kentucky and babysat her and she picked it up from being in their presence." Ria still has that drawl.

What is it that you've picked up somewhere in life that might be a liability to you? What fears, what beliefs that you're holding on to tenaciously that no longer allow your life to work?

They are not helping you to produce the results that you want, yet you're still clinging to them. As we enter into a new world, there are some old behaviors that just won't fit. What are the events? What are the circumstances? Who are the people that have shaped you? Just keep thinking, questioning, and examining. What are the things you need to let go of? Are there things that have caused you pain, that are stifling your growth and development? Look at your profession or career and ask what you need to do to upgrade your knowledge and skills to be competitive in the marketplace. Begin to look at yourself, spend time, and ask these questions. What is something you're good at? Are you living your passion? Are you living your dream? What do you regard as your greatest personal achievement? What is the one thing that other people can do to make you most happy?

Let's think about these things. What would you do if you had one year to live and were guaranteed success in anything you decided to do? What would that be? What would you do with your life if you had it to live over? Just thinking, getting to know yourself. What is one value, one deep commitment from which you would never budge? What is one cause that you would like to become involved with to make a difference on the planet? I work in the Cook County Jail in Chicago. It gives my life a great deal of joy and fulfillment. Have you found something like that in your life that you could enjoy doing? Working with people or for a cause?

I have a friend who used to be constantly depressed and who was always feeling sorry for herself, who began working with physically handicapped people. It's been the most rewarding experience she's ever had. It has changed her life. She's a grateful person. She's found something that she's lost herself in.

Spend time thinking, just thinking. What is your biggest setback, failure, or defeat of the past year? What is it about you that if somebody really knew, they wouldn't get into a relationship with you?

Once you acknowledge these things in your life, start working on them and change them. It's easy to blame the other person, but you need to start taking ownership for where you are. Are you proud of how you have been living your life? Have you explored your natural talents and your gifts by enthusiastically trying a variety of activities? A lot of us have so much talent, so many abilities, yet we put them on the back burner, leaving them behind. We never did anything with them, never brought them out. Something you used to do extremely well in high school or college or just a natural gift, yet you never did anything with it.

What gifts are you sitting on? Have you resigned yourself to a life feeling that nothing can be done to change your future or your circumstances? Have you been afraid to try something different because you're afraid of how people will react to you or what they will think? These are some of the questions that I suggest you begin to answer.

Here are some things that you need to begin to work on to develop your character. These character-building activities will give you some personal strength. Webster's says that character is the pattern of behavior, of personality found in an individual or group; moral strength, self-discipline, fortitude. Character is what's going to be required in order to manifest your greatness. As you begin looking at yourself, ask what are the things you need to be in the process of doing more of or less of? Let's look at some I've spent time with.

It was very difficult for me to say no without feeling guilty.

I found it very challenging to be direct. I used to have the problem of not telling people what I actually thought because I didn't want to hurt anybody's feelings.

I wanted to be more focused. I used to do a lot of things. I was a jack of all trades and master of none.

One year, I decided to do one thing well. I looked at all of my talents and I decided the strongest one was my ability as a speaker and that's the one I'm going to focus on. I'm capable of doing a lot of other things, but only when I decided to focus on one did I begin to reap the rewards of my talents.

Decide to keep your word. Just say, "I'm going to keep my word. If I say something, I'm going to do it regardless."

Look at your life and find the things that you can say, "Hey, I know I've got a problem in this area." Try being more considerate, more trusting, more disciplined. Try being less fearful, more adventurous.

Being late. I need to take care of that. Procrastinating, I need to deal with that. Not taking care of business. Being seriously not serious. Creating an imbalance in my life where I'm spending more time looking at television or having social fun and not spending enough time working on me. Many people spend more time working on their jobs than they spend working on themselves. Whatever we achieve in life, whatever we create, whatever we're able to manifest, comes out of the human mind.

I want you to think about five things that would give you a feeling of satisfaction and self-respect if you had the courage to do them. Take the time to write these things down, whatever they might be. It might

be in your personal life. It might be in your friend-
ships, or your family relationships. It might be in your
business.

I was negotiating with a friend of mine that I admire
a great deal, and she went back on her agreement and
I did not challenge her on it. Number one was because
of my admiration for her. Number two, because I really
wanted the business and I think she sensed that, so I
didn't want to seem too picky. I was nervous about it
and I was cowardly because I should have said, "Listen,
that's not what we agreed to." I should have called her
on that, but I didn't want to look bad or to appear to be
negative or risk losing the business.

Look at those five things that if you had the courage
to do, you would do. A lot of people say, "Well, I've been
like this all my life, I just can't change that. This is the
way I am." Dr. Harold Greenwald, a psychologist and
author of *Direct Decision Therapy* said, "When someone
says I can't change, some part of them wants to change,
but the payoffs for his present behavior are greater
than the payoffs for a changed behavior, or his fear of
change is too great."

It takes courage to live your dreams. It takes courage to manifest your greatness. It takes courage to
decide to live, to decide to bring out all of your talents
and abilities, to decide to stretch out, to decide to take
a chance. It takes courage to be happy just to be you.

I saw a friend who I hadn't seen for a long time. Her whole personality has changed. She was an extroverted, assertive person, but now because her husband has a fragile ego when she's around him, she plays to him. She's very silent. She doesn't express herself or her true feelings. There are many things she wants to do, but won't make a decision without checking with him. How will he handle this? How will he see this? Will this be disruptive in our relationship? A lot of us, both men and women, readjust our behavior and end up not being who we really are in deference to relationships.

Looking at the word courage, Webster says, "The attitude of facing and dealing with anything recognized as dangerous, difficult or painful, instead of withdrawing from it." As you begin to look at where you want to go and take personal inventory, it's going to be very uncomfortable. That's why most people don't do it. It's very painful to admit your shortcomings and your weaknesses. It's very painful to do that. It's much easier to withdraw, and just ignore them.

It goes on to having the courage of one's convictions, the courage to do what one thinks is right. As you begin to look at yourself and where you want to go with your life, it's very important to ask yourself this question: Is what you are doing right now giving you what you want? If it's not giving you what you want, it's going to take courage to decide to do something differently. It takes courage to enjoy yourself. What are some of the self-defeating behaviors that we become involved in that prevent us from enjoying ourselves? Some people develop the 'what's-the-use' attitude. Why bother? Some people have the 'I-really-don't-care' attitude. They convince themselves that they don't care and they don't feel anything, and after a while, they really don't feel anything. Their lives are empty. Some people say, "Well, it's really not worth the hassle. That's too hard. It doesn't bother me anymore, the fact that I'm not living out my dream. The fact that I'm capable of doing more but I'm not doing it. The fact that I'm content but I'm not fulfilled. The fact that I'm not living my dream."

In their book, *I Want to Change But I Don't Know How,* Tom Rusk and Randy Read said, "People go through life many times playing it safe. That's the secret hope that they say to themselves. If I never let myself feel too good maybe I'll never get hurt too badly."

Often people don't do the things they're capable of because they allow themselves to go along with the crowd, or to follow the crowd. Many people have things they want to do but they find themselves in relationships with people who are addicted to mediocrity and they allow themselves to be influenced by their behavior. Many people allow their lack of self-confidence to immobilize them. I wanted to go into business for years. It was an agonizing thought in my mind. I wouldn't try it because I didn't believe that I could make it.

Of the five things that you would like to do if you had the courage to, I want you to pick one. Here's how to set it up for yourself to help free you and get you unstuck. Ask yourself, what is the worst thing that can happen if you do it? What's the worst thing? Let's say, going into business for yourself or changing careers, or getting a divorce. Taking some kind of chance on something you've always thought about doing but you just haven't done it for whatever reason. What's the worst thing that can happen, the worst-case scenario?

When you have the worst-case scenario, write it down. Write down the worst things that you fear could happen. Naming your fears puts you in control. What are you afraid of? Name it. Write it out, so you can look at it. Confront that fear. What is it?

"I'm afraid that things might work out?"

"What else?"

"Well, I've never been in business, okay?"

"What else?"

"Well, I don't have all the help I need."

"Okay, good. What else?"

"Well, I don't have enough money, all right?"

"Good. What else?"

"Well, I don't have a college degree."

"I'm not as good as those other guys that I've seen up there speaking."

"Okay, what else?"

"Well, that's all I can think of right now."

"Okay, good."

This takes you to the next step. What are the benefits? What are the benefits of your acting courageously, of taking life on? Part of what happened for me was that I felt better within myself, and I had a strong sense of self-respect. I made a lot of mistakes going into business for myself. Sometimes I was down on myself. I felt stupid. I felt dumb because people who were in business said, "Why would you do something like that?" "Well, I didn't know." "Boy, you were really dumb," and I used to chime in with, "Yes, I guess I was." I didn't know any better, but the other thing is, I had to say to myself, "But I did it. I did it even if I made a flop of it, I did it." I took the chance. I took the leap.

What are the benefits of your acting courageously? Whatever you've identified, write those benefits down, and then focus on them. Focus on the benefits, not on the liabilities, not on your fears. Focus on the benefits since that which you hold in consciousness tends to manifest itself. Think about how good you'd feel. Think about the increase in self-respect, the sense of self-worth, how good you will feel getting up in the morning, looking yourself in the mirror, because you're taking life on.

The next thing is to acknowledge your fears and then go into action. I like the book by Susan Jeffers, *Feel the Fear and Do It Anyway*. That says it all. I believe anybody who's ever taken a chance, who's ever done anything, doesn't mean that they are not afraid. Courageous does not mean the absence of fear. Being courageous is being willing to do it anyway, because that's what you feel. You do it regardless of the fear. You're not going to be immobilized by your fears or your doubts. You admit, "Okay, I'm scared to death now. Okay, what is it that I must choose to do?" Go ahead and experience that fear but don't let that fear stop you.

In what you've done with your life thus far, is it giving you what you want? When you look toward the future, when you look at all that's going on out there, is there some voice within saying, "Hey, I know I need to be out there in that arena. I know I can do more than what I've been doing. I know there's some great music that I have within me that I haven't brought out." Is that something that you begin to look at within yourself? I used to do that and I used to go to big rallies and see guys up speaking when I wasn't courageous enough to go out there and say, "Hey, my name is Les Brown, the motivator, Mamie Brown's boy. I want to talk." I would never do that. I'd just be back there looking at them and wanting to get their autograph. "Can I meet Mr. Zig Ziglar? Please tell him." "Who are you?" "Les Brown." Because I felt within myself that I was a nobody so who am I to go talk to these great speakers and get their autographs, and admit, "I'd like to do what you do."

I say if you look at your life and if you're not getting what you want, you owe it to yourself to do something differently. I've heard that eighty-five percent of Americans go to jobs where they say they're unhappy. If you're doing something eight hours a day that you don't like, then it's not giving you what you want, it's not giving you a strong feeling of satisfaction and fulfillment. You are miserable, you hate to go there, you're depressed just thinking about it, and you sing the 'Thank God it's Friday' song every week. It's giving you headaches just thinking about it on Sunday afternoon after the game. If that's your life, you owe it to yourself to start strategically working to change directions.

Most people, however, will resist change. Most people will fight change as if change would be worse than what they are experiencing. *This*, they know *this*. They are familiar with *this*. Most people will not challenge the unknown. They won't just step out there. "Well, see, there's certain things that's got to be in place." They got to see it all together and life isn't like that. That's not how you grow. As you look at your life, are you saying "I'm not getting what I want?" As you begin to look toward the future, begin to know that whatever it takes for you to create that, you've got that in you. You've got genius in you, you've got goodness in you, you've got creativity in you. If you decide to take the initiative to change the current quality of your life, I think that you will find that the universe is on your side. That *life* is on your side.

Will it be turbulent? Yes. Will it be easy? No. Will you have some opposition? Yes. Will I make a lot of mistakes? Yes. Will I get hurt? Yes. Many people won't try anything different in life because they don't want to get hurt. Let me tell you something, pain is everywhere. You can hide over there but it will find you. Viktor Frankl calls it unavoidable suffering. You can't avoid it yet most people spend their lives not wanting to deal with the pain of rejection, the pain of defeat, the pain of being disappointed, the pain of losing, the pain of failure, the pain of being criticized, the pain of not being liked, the pain, the pain, the pain. That's called life. Life is full of pain. It's everywhere. But guess what, there's no gain without pain. And the pain of regret is also real. I think if we're all going to suffer pain in our lives anyway, we might as well get something out of it.

I was in a seminar and the topic came to "If I had my life to live over again." One woman stood up and shared all of the things that she would do differently, and you could feel the pain of regret in her voice. She still experienced pain. She was trying not to experience the pain of defeat, the pain of disappointment, the pain of loss, the pain of lack of support, and she still experienced pain. It was right there. We can't get around it.

Most people are governed by their habits, their fears, and the opinions of others. Many would never try anything different because the people they value in their lives have them convinced that they can't do it. They're living within the context of other people's opinions of them, of other people's low expectations. It is easy to doubt yourself when your previous experience is that at some critical point, somebody they respected, honored, and believed in, somebody that they loved, someone they trusted said, "You can't do that," and they accepted it.

That's why I didn't go to college. I believed a teacher who said, "You're not college material, Mr. Brown. You're not as smart as your brother, Wesley, or your sister, Margaret Ann. Why don't you try and get a job at the post office? Try and do something with your hands or look for a job with the sanitation department." I had already failed the test to get into the Army, so I went down to the sanitation department because that's what I believed was possible for me. As you look at your life, ask yourself the question, what would your life be like? What would your life look like if you decided not to care what people thought of you? What would your life be like if you decided to give up some of your fears? What would your life be like if you decided to become courageous? What would your life be like if you decided to act on your dream, if you did what you felt in your heart?

Do you know what courageous means? In their book *I Want to Change but I Don't Know How*, Tom Rusk and Randy Read talk about courage. The word comes from the French meaning "of the heart." They say, "It takes courage to live." Most people go through life not allowing themselves to step out because they don't want to let go. They don't want to be blown around. They don't want to be moved. It takes courage to face life's whirling wind of contradictions, courage to love yourself, courage to love others, courage to take a chance, courage to be who you are.

They say, "Courage isn't for somebody else, for medals, applause, or moral debts. Courage is what, at that moment, feels most right for you, not just situational ethics, but what feels right in your heart. The word of the heart, what feels right in *your* heart." Shakespeare said, "Cowards die many times before their deaths. The valiant never taste of death but once." What does that mean? That valiant people aren't afraid? No. It means they experience that fear, and they move forward anyway. They move forward.

By allowing their dreams to die, many are already tolerating lives of slow death. So many are allowing their ideas to lie dormant and collect dust. Without the courage to be who they truly are, all their talents and abilities are buried inside of them, and will go with them to their graves.

As you look toward the future and begin to manifest your greatness, it's going to take everything in you. Your life deserves your concentrated effort. Begin to ask yourself these questions. How can I express more of *me*? How can I bring *my* ideas out here now? Start living with a sense of urgency because you're here today, you're here now.

Life is unpredictable. It's uncertain. There are no guarantees, no guarantees out here at all. Ask yourself, what's the benefit of waiting? What's the benefit of not living your dream? What's the benefit of not listening to yourself? Please listen to yourself.

Start listening to the feelings in your heart. I'm doing it more every day and finding I can trust my feelings more and more. As you look toward the future, and begin to look at life on a daily basis, don't allow that inner doubt in you to take over. If you've heard something within yourself, if you realize that what you're doing now doesn't work for you, doesn't fit, is not giving you what you want, and there's something else that you want to do, don't let that inner doubt talk you out of it. Don't let your doubts build a case for why you can't have it or tell you why you're not good enough.

Learn to ignore that inner voice and all of the external voices. Don't judge the possibilities for what you can do based upon the circumstances, because the circumstances won't determine who you are. Circumstances don't determine what you're able to do based upon your resources. Circumstances can't determine what's possible for you, based upon where your life is right now. Where your life is right now is not you. That's just what it is right now. The possibilities for you are unlimited. If you're in a rebuilding process, it's unlimited. If you're coming back from adversity and devastation, it's unlimited as to what you can do.

That's the capacity of human beings. It doesn't matter how many mistakes you've made, doesn't matter how many flops you've had, doesn't matter how much money you've lost. In fact, I see those not as losses, but as investments in life lessons, learning what's possible for you. Once you start listening to yourself, and as you begin to act on your dreams, as you start just trying to find your way doing what you can, with what you have, you will start seeing things opening up for you. You'll start attracting people. You will say, "Where did this come from?" Things will start coming together and start clicking for you.

You'll start brainstorming. Ideas will come out of nowhere as you focus. The key is to learn to focus on what it is you want to do. This is important because that which we focus on, that which we give our energy to, will begin to multiply. It will begin to expand. You will begin to develop your consciousness and out of that comes your greatness, out of that comes a commitment, out of that comes a passion for life, out of that comes a special power that you have in you, that you haven't even called on yet. The powers that we have will never reveal themselves if we don't challenge them, if we don't put ourselves in situations where we have to use them.

In his book, *Instant Millionaire*, Mark Fisher says, "Put yourself in a position where you can't retreat, where it's do or die, sink or swim." Here's what you'll find out. You'll develop incredible swimming skills or swallow half the pool of life. You'll find yourself swimming like you've never done before. Through the inspiration of desperation, you'll become more creative than ever before. So what is it? How do we handle that whole piece? Throw your whole self into it. Most people go at it tentatively. They don't concentrate. They don't put everything they've got into it. In his book, *All You Can Do Is All You Can Do but All You Can Do Is Enough*, A.L. Williams said, "Make sure you do all you can do."

When we are honest with ourselves, we know that we haven't done all we can do. As we look ahead, we can decide that from this day forward, we will do all we can do to develop ourselves, to bring our talents out here, to make a contribution to life.

You've got greatness within you. As you look toward the future in developing your greatness, begin to know that your life is worth the effort. Is it easy? No. Is it worth it? Yes, yes, yes! Your life is worth it and so are you.

CHAPTER 12

The Power of Self-Approval

Self-approval is a very challenging area. Why is it challenging? That's where many people get stuck. Many factors can contribute to our not feeling good enough. Many of us never had anybody to believe in us. That makes it very challenging to develop good feelings about ourselves, to bring out our talents and make a contribution to life.

We've all done some things that we don't feel good about, that if we had to do over we would do differently, or not do at all. In order to grow and begin to move into our greatness, let's look at and prepare to remove this major energy block around the issue of forgiveness.

Start by making a list. It will be a long list. Here are things to think about and put on your list: things you've done that you feel bad about, that you regret, and people that have hurt you, someone who's done you wrong or that you have hurt. There may be a time when you weren't a good father, a good mother, a good brother or a sister or you were a bad child, you didn't do a good job, you lied, you were dishonest. Also put on the list some things you feel good about that you've done.

All of us have some good and some bad. Martin Luther King said, "There is some good in the worst of us and some bad in the best of us." None of us have escaped.

One of the first steps in this process is to remove the clutter from your life. I want you to become involved in an active process to de-clutter all parts of your life. Start working on any areas in your life that you need to clean up. I started with my closets. The first law of the universe is order. Go home and clean up your closets. Get the clutter out. Start letting some of this junk go to make some room for something else.

There are some people who are cluttering up your life. They are no longer serving any purpose for you and are occupying space that somebody useful, positive, nurturing, and contributing might hold. If you're surrounded by people that are not helping you to grow you won't even have time to explore and develop new possibilities.

Ask yourself, "What is it I need to get out of my life?" and then just start cleaning this stuff out. There are the closets, the dressers, the drawers, the desk, and don't forget the car. Whatever you have in your environment is a reflection of your consciousness. Living with clutter and chaos represents some disorganized, cluttered section of your mind. Work to get that out. Clean that up.

Next, let's look at anybody you feel very strongly about—have some negative feelings about—and let's look at some good reasons to forgive them. Number one, try and see clearly what has happened or to see things from their point of view. Number two, holding a grudge hurts you. It doesn't hurt them. Just for good health and peace of mind, let it go. Any feeling of resentment, anger, or hatred has called to me the load of bitterness within.

Every thought we entertain produces a chemical in our brain that impacts our body's immune system. Besides, this person you hate, they probably are not even aware of it. They could be someplace having a good time and don't even know you hate them. You've turned up the steam—gone from dislike to hate. Here you are killing yourself, making yourself vulnerable to various types of illnesses, putting yourself in bad health. That person is not worth sacrificing your health or one minute of peace of mind. One minute of anger robs you of sixty seconds of happiness.

Decide it doesn't matter. Let it go and experience the dignity and the magnanimous sense of character of being big enough to move on and get on with your life. Let it go so you can grow.

Now let's think about this lack of self-acceptance. How does it show up? How does it manifest itself? All of us have greatness within us, but when you don't come to grips with your greatness and you don't work to develop it—if you're not seeking it out, if you're not finding where it is, if you're not trying to locate it, if you're not experimenting with your life to try and find out what fits for you—you're positioning yourself to be a miserable and an unfulfilled person.

How else do we avoid self-acceptance? Procrastination. We just put things off over and over and over again. Why? We don't feel deserving. We don't feel that we are good enough. We sabotage ourselves by not ever taking care of business. We get real busy doing a lot of things but we don't have any time. In his book, *University of Success,* Og Mandino said, "Many of us never, ever discover our greatness because we become sidetracked by secondary activity." We start doing so many things; we just give our time away until we don't have any time for ourselves or any time to do the things that we really want to do.

Think about every time you put it off and move it back, "Oh, I'll do it one day. Oh yeah. I'm going to get to it." One day you'll look around and there goes a year, there goes two years, there goes three years. If there's something you want to do, do it now. Do it right now. Don't put it off. Start right now, where you are. There will never be a perfect ideal time. Whatever you have going for you right now, that's enough. Work on that idea. Work on it, work on it, work on it.

Another way in which lack of self-acceptance shows up is in the relationships we form, the people we have around us. This reminds me of two young men I've known. Larry Little was a football player at Booker T. Washington High School—where I graduated from—and went to Bethune-Cookman College. Larry became an all-star offensive guard playing for the Miami Dolphins, and is an all-around great guy. But Larry wasn't really the most talented guy in that position at Booker T. Washington High School.

Willie Covington was a far more talented player at Booker T. He was faster and physically stronger. But Willie never made it out of high school. He started running with the wrong crowd and those people led him to the penitentiary and ultimately, to a premature death.

Willie Covington had great talent and great potential, but was running with the wrong crowd. Watch out for the relationships you have.

What kind of person are you becoming because of the relationships that you have right now? Do those people contribute to you? Do they help you grow and develop yourself? What kind of person are you becoming? People who have not accepted greatness for themselves don't study. They don't have time for personal growth and development. They don't have time to work on their minds. They don't have time for that. They're too busy for that.

People can affect us, our peers can affect us, and our environment can affect us. I have been intentionally working to overcome the poverty consciousness that I was raised in, constantly saying to myself, "Les Brown, you deserve this. There's no need for you to be afraid." It's not too good to be true. It's true because you've earned it the old-fashioned way. You have worked for it. Every once in a while, it comes up when I at least expect it. My heart starts beating fast and I start questioning myself, doubting myself, and I catch myself. You've got to be consciously conscious.

Let's look at how we can begin to evaluate our self-esteem, our self-approval. Number one, to determine the height of your self-approval, it's important that you evaluate yourself but it's almost impossible to do it entirely by yourself. You must get some caring feedback. Find somebody close enough to you that has observed you, has been around you, whose opinion you value, and ask: how do they see you, how do they rate you in terms of your self-esteem? Compare what's on your list with what they say.

There are things that people can see in us that we can't see, because it's a blind spot for us. If I'm talking to you and my breath is offensive and you don't tell me, then I'm unaware but you and everyone else around is aware. All you have to do is just tell me, "Les, you need to gargle or something."

We all have those blind spots. We have those areas of our lives that we need to get some caring feedback. We need some coaching. We need someone to let us know. Why don't people just volunteer this feedback? They don't want to hurt your feelings. They don't want to embarrass you. Some simply don't want to hear it and are likely to argue or become defensive. If you're one of those people, just decide to shut up and listen.

How well do you handle compliments? This is a good barometer to check out how you feel about yourself. When someone pays you a compliment, can you handle it well? I said to a woman out in our hallway, "Oh, what a beautiful dress you have." She replied, "Oh, it's nothing, I got it on sale. It's nothing." Now, I didn't ask if she got it on sale? I just said was a beautiful dress. Can you handle compliments well? That's a good barometer about your self-esteem. Can you handle criticism well? Can you give criticism?

What are your expectations? What do you expect to get from life? What do you expect to get from your business? What do you expect to get from your relationships? What is your ideal day? What is it that you expect from this experience, this trip, this journey that you're involved in? People who have a strong sense of self-approval have high expectations for themselves, from life and from others. A lot of people don't expect much from life, so they don't shoot for much, they're not preparing for much.

A lot of people are just showing up in life. They get up in the morning and go through the day watching the clock. They go to the job just to get the check. You want to be a different kind of person as you go forward. You want to get something out of this. If you're going to do it, it's worth your time, your energy. You've got some expectations from this. I do not let people waste my time. If someone wants to meet with me, I want to know why and if it does not measure up to my expectations, I'm not going to invest my time. I don't have the luxury to waste time. I'm expecting some great things from my life and I plan to spend time working on and developing myself. Examine your expectations versus your wishes.

Some people wish they could do better but some people expect to do better. Where are you on that?

Let's look at what things we can do to increase our self-approval, our self-appreciation, our self-acceptance. Number one, love yourself. Make caring for yourself the highest priority in your life. Take care of you; look out for what truly satisfies you. We are not taught to love ourselves. We are not taught to look out for ourselves. We are not taught to take care of ourselves—to become sensitive to our wants, our needs, or our desires. Make a conscious effort. Make *you* your number one priority. Your peace of mind, your health, is more important than anyone because without peace of mind or your health, you can't serve anyone.

Don't neglect yourself. A lot of us, particularly women, have been groomed to be sacrificial lambs, putting their dreams on the back burner in deference to their children's dreams, their husband's dreams or their family's dreams. They forget about themselves and become resentful, angry, and bitter. Start taking care of yourself, looking out for you. Develop a health plan. Your health is all you have. Start taking care of you.

Start by taking care of your body—loving yourself starts here. Eat delicious and nutritious meals and be willing to exercise. Do some good stuff for yourself on purpose. Take some time out for you. I have some good things I enjoy doing for myself. One is taking spiritual baths. I play my favorite music. I have different oils that I put in a tub of hot water. I sprinkle flowers that I've picked in the water, and I soak. The flowers remind me of scenes of Eddie Murphy in the movie *Coming to America* where they would sprinkle flowers on the ground. The flowers give me a feeling of royalty. I soak and sometimes read or just relax, enjoy the music and just cool out. That's my time for me. I turn off the phone. I just block out some time for me.

You can't develop and manifest your greatness; you can't be a high achiever, if you don't feel good. I'm taking care of me. I've been working out and exercising. I've just been doing some things for me, taking care of myself mentally, emotionally, spiritually, and physically. I'm into meditation. You know what? All this attention and care takes the edge off your life. It helps you to manage things rather than allowing them to manage you. It gives you more personal power to deal with stuff. To take care of you.

Here's something else I suggest. Become aware of what your needs are and develop compassion towards yourself despite your human defects. You will never be perfect. You're human. You've made a lot of mistakes. You've done a lot of dumb, stupid things. Guess what, you're not through yet. You're going to do some more. Hurry up and get it over with. It's all right. You have got to learn to be gentle with yourself.

Make it all right. What you don't know, mistakes that you make—it's okay. Handle it. Learn from the experience. Decide that you are going to do whatever you become involved in, to be upfront, to be true to yourself. Are you getting what you need out of it? Be upfront with people and tell them what you need from them. Don't assume that they know. Don't say, "I thought you knew." No, tell people upfront. Here's what I need from this, in order for this to work for me. Be upfront with your stuff. Tell them upfront, so they are not surprised later and know what to expect.

If you don't take care of your needs, you will always have that nagging thought in the back of your mind saying, "When do I get mine? When am I going to start enjoying this?" We're taught to be quiet and not speak up for ourselves and not to be selfish. If you don't take care of you, who do you think is going to do it? Who's going to look out for you better than you will? No one. No one is going to do that.

No one's going to take care of your business better than you. Nobody. Anything you want to do in life, you've got to take ownership of it and say, "Hey, I'm going to make this happen." Be willing to venture out and do something that you have fantasized about doing. You know you probably won't be good at it but do it anyhow.

The next thing is to learn to avoid people and situations that upset you. There are some people that know just how to push your buttons; they know just what to say. I've learned it's best to just avoid them. You might call that cowardly but I don't want to expend my energy like that. Life is too short and unpredictable. I don't want to spend my time arguing with, or being irritated by, anybody. I've learned to avoid situations and things that will get me upset.

I don't watch movies that frighten me. The last frightening movie I saw was *The Exorcist*. I never watched another one after that. It was two weeks before I could sleep with the lights out. I only watch comedies; things that make me laugh, make me feel good, make me feel like the little boy in me. Life is just too serious.

Here's something else that can help to increase your self-esteem. Draw the line. There are certain things that we just put up with and at some point, we've got to draw the line and just say, "Enough is enough." Learn to do that with yourself. Just draw the line.

I've learned to do this with myself. I get on the scale every day. If I get to a certain number, that's a crisis and I just get down and start doing sit-ups right there, right then. If my income would drop to a certain level, I would start working like crazy, making 200 calls a day. These are some of the lines I've drawn for myself.

There are certain things that you just don't permit. You've got to draw a line. Negative people in your life can be very challenging but this is very important. I had someone I loved very much, but finally had the courage to say, "I love you very much. But if you're persistent in saying those kinds of things to me, I'm saying to you right now I won't tolerate that. I will have to terminate this because I'm not going to expose myself to this type of humiliation. I don't like getting called names and putting each other down. I don't like that." It may seem cold. Maybe it is, but I've learned it's best to get people out of my life that aren't good for me.

One negative stroke is sixteen times more powerful than a positive stroke. If you have people around you who are not sensitive to who you are then it's time to leave them behind. Often the people that can hurt you the most are the people that you love and are most vulnerable to. They're the ones who can get to you. Yet I don't care who they are. If you don't draw the line and you just let them run rampant in your life, if you let things happen to you that you don't feel good about, and if you continue to allow it to happen, you won't feel good about yourself. You will not grow. Your image of yourself will erode, so you've got to draw the line.

Why are known hells preferable to strange heavens? Why do people just go to a job where they're miserable day in and day out? Why do people stay together even though they are miserable; sleeping in separate rooms or always arguing? The only thing they have in common is paying the bills. They don't talk, they don't communicate, and they don't share anything together day in and day out. As short and unpredictable that life is, why are people so mean to each other?

Known hells are preferable to strange heavens because they are familiar. Life is rough and it is scary. It's scary growing, it's scary taking a chance, it's scary acting on your intuition, on your guts. It's scary, it's frightening. There are people who are just tolerating things right now and they're immobilized by fear. Journalist and historian Theodore White said, "To go against the dominant thinking of your family, friends, and those people you associate with every day is perhaps the most difficult act of courage you will ever perform." When you start growing, when you start changing the way you walk, the way you talk, the way you act, the way you respond to things, the way you use your time, your self-confidence and awareness will blossom. Start drawing the line for yourself, start with saying, "No, I can't do that." "Why? You don't have the time?" "No. I have my own agenda. I've got something that I'm doing." You are not lying or just trying to get out of it. Just say, "I'm busy doing something that I want to do," or "I'm not mad, or upset. I just don't want to do it." Why? "I don't want to do it. Thank you so much for asking me." Don't let people try to put a guilt trip on you. You have to draw the line.

Don't go through life feeling like you're powerless. Don't let yourself be a victim of people that are powerless. You're not powerless. You are powerful. You direct the power in your life. Whatever your life is right now it is a duplication of your consciousness. It's a result of how you have decided to use your power. That's all it is. That's not who you are. That's just a perverted use of your power that you aren't satisfied with and you've got the power to change that. Wherever you are, I don't know how but I know you've got the power to do that. "You don't know what has happened to me." It really doesn't matter what has happened to you. The only thing that really matters is, what are you going to do about it now? That's all that matters. You can allow it to destroy you or you can allow it to build you up.

In his book, *Why I'm Afraid to Tell You Who I Am,* John Powell recounts a story of his going out to get a newspaper. The clerk was very rude to him yet he remained very courteous to the clerk. His companion asked, "Why would you be so courteous to this guy considering how rude he was to you?" He answered, "I'm not going to allow that man to determine how I'm going to act." Things are going to happen to you in life. Make it okay. As the serenity prayer says, "Lord, grant me the serenity to accept the things that I cannot change." I cannot change the fact that when I asked my son to move out he became angry and perhaps hated my guts. "To change the things that I can." I can change how I respond to it. I can become upset, nervous, tense about it, weak about it or I can say, "It's okay. I am doing the right thing for me." Become comfortable with it.

What's the next thing? Learn something new and tackle it in a spirit of adventure and love. Somebody said that we are not stricken by the things we do but we are stricken by the things that we don't do, the songs that have not been sung, the poems we have not written, the work we have not done, the ideas we have not developed, the dreams we have not acted on. That's what constricted you and can block your power. That's what can rob you of peace, satisfaction, self-respect, and this special joy you can get out of life with special achievement.

One thing that contributes to high self-acceptance is self-achievement. It feels great when you achieve something and you can stand back, look at it, and say "I did this." What if it doesn't work out? You can stand back, look at it and say, "I tried it. I went for it. It didn't work out. I value the experience. I loved just the experience of doing it. I love that."

That's why I said, "I've been fantasizing about singing. I'm going to do this. Who says that when I first stand up and sing I have to sound like Pavarotti? I can sound like Les. That's right. Mamie Brown's boy." Look at your life and find something that you can tackle and do it with love, something that you love. When you do that, you're doing it in a spirit of love.

I know that there is greatness in you. I know there is something in you. Everybody has something. As you focus, as you go into action, as you hold that thought in consciousness persistently, you begin to develop the consciousness to manifest and create all kinds of things. You will begin to realize powers and abilities you have.

When you walk into the room people will say, "I don't know what it is but there's something different about you. There's just something about the way you look. It's a glow but what is it? What are you doing now?" "I'm just being who I am. I'm just living out my greatness. I'm approving myself and giving myself permission to pursue my dream."

It's there. I know it's there. Give yourself permission to realize all the powers and abilities you have. Pursue your dreams. Pursue your greatness.

CHAPTER 13

The Power of Commitment

Commitment shows up in your life through action. You can tell people who are committed and those people who don't feel worthy. The people that are committed are busy doing it. Then there are the people who don't feel worthy. The guy I talked to last night told me, "Hey, I sure would like to do what you're doing. However, I just don't want the responsibility. The company I work for, they're taking good care of me." I said, "Let me tell you something. Once you increase your sense of worthiness, you won't even be able to open your mouth saying that somebody is taking care of you. You want to take care of yourself."

He doesn't feel worthy, but he's intelligent. He has worked seventeen years for a major corporation that has spent thousands of dollars training him. He knows he has the book knowledge, but his attitude, his vision of himself, his sense of deservingness says, "You can't have that." He will fabricate all kinds of excuses why he can't have it. Management theorist Robert Anthony said, "You can only have two things in life, reasons and results. Notice reasons don't count." I like that.

Folks will always point out reasons why they're not living their dream, why they're not manifesting their greatness. They will always be able to point those things out but none of those things count. Results are the only thing that count and results don't lie. They tell it all. Judge a tree by the fruit that it bears, not the ones it might talk about, not the ones that it might wish for, think about, or affirm but the fruit that it actually bears.

Let's look at this. I think that all of us are committed, since I don't think that as a participant in life you can be uncommitted. You're either committed to mediocrity or you're committed to greatness. You're either committed to being productive or you're committed to being non-productive. You're committed to being happy or you're committed to being unhappy. Whatever you're doing, however you spend your time, that tells you who you are. Think about what it is you like to create in your life experience. Once I look at how you commit your time, how you spend your time, I can tell you exactly what you're committed to.

People say they have dreams. They want to open a business or want to do something differently than what they're doing now. They don't like their jobs, they're unhappy, they're unfulfilled. They want to improve their income level. Look at how they spend their time, the commitment of their time. How they use that time will tell the truth. People say, "I'd like to do better," but you don't find them upgrading their skills and their knowledge in vocational or technical schools.

How they spend their time will tell you what's going on. People say they want to normalize their weight, they want to be healthy, but every time you see them, they're eating. That tells you they're committed to being obese for the rest of their lives. People tell you they want to stop smoking while they're lighting up. Folks who say, "I want to stop drinking," and then every time you're in their face, they're reeking with alcohol. That tells you what's going on. Don't listen to what they say. Just watch what they do. Commitment shows up in what you do.

On the other hand, you can make the commitment to your life, and if you don't like where you are, you can decide you're going to do something about it. That power is available to all of us. People look at life and decide, "I want something different for myself."

Carol, a single mother living in Detroit, decided that she wanted to open her own business, a health food store, but did not have enough money to do it. She sold her car and used the money to get started in a little hole in the wall storefront. She rode to work on a bicycle. Then, when she got enough money, she bought a motor scooter and did that for a long time. She is now a very successful business owner with three health food stores. She said, "It was hard. It was a struggle, Les, but I did it. I made the commitment to do it and I did it."

Why is it that people are frightened by commitment? The word commitment intimidates a lot of people. Why? Because it means you have to deliver. Many folks, if you say to them, "I would like you to do this," they will say, "I'll try." "I'll try" means that is my escape clause when I don't come through. It's really a polite no. I don't have the courage to tell you no, so I'll tell you I tried. "Hey, look. I need you to come to this meeting." "I'll try." "What do you mean? You're going to lean toward the meeting?" Try and sit down. You either do or you don't. Try and take this pencil out of my hand. You either do or you don't. There's no such thing as try.

Most people like to use that language. They don't want to commit themselves because commitment means among many things, no excuse is acceptable. That's what it means, no excuse. If you decided you want to do something and it becomes hard, then do it hard. If it's difficult, so what? If it's inconvenient, so what? That's how people lose their way following their dreams. They don't honor their commitment to themselves.

Let me tell you what happens when you don't keep your commitment. Number one, it begins to deplete your self-esteem and it erodes your self-image. It weakens your faith in yourself. You don't feel good when you don't keep your commitments. The other thing is that you begin to develop weak relationships with people. People begin to realize they can't depend upon you. They can't rely on you because you won't keep your word.

You've established that kind of reputation. Just think, what would your life be like if you decided to keep your commitments? What will all of our lives be like if we decided to keep our commitments, to do the things that we said that we were going to do, that we wouldn't even speak it unless we were going to do it? Let's decide that for just one week to see what your life can be like. Let's make a commitment, a seven-day commitment that we won't say we will do anything unless we're willing and able to do it.

Do this and find out what your life will be like. Let me tell you that if you follow through, if you keep your commitment to the commitment, at the end of the seven days you'll feel strong and powerful. By honoring your commitment you will immediately discover the discipline and resolve that is required, and you will find yourself focuses and empowered.

I'm suggesting that first of all, you commit yourself to live in the present. I was very moved by the scene in the movie, *The Dead Poets Society,* with Robin Williams as the teacher, who tells his students "carpe diem" which means "seize the day." Many of us are not able to develop and manifest our greatness because we spend so much time looking back or worrying about the future. Seize the moment. You cannot go into the future and manifest your greatness when you have various things in your life blocking you.

Let's look at how we can begin to keep our commitments. Dr. Robert Anthony said this about results, "When you keep your commitments, you're able to produce some different kinds of results in your life." How can we keep our commitments, and do we keep all commitments? No, we don't. You will not be at one hundred percent. However, you will have a greater percentage rate of maintaining your commitments to yourself, whatever those things might be. If it's going into business, if it's changing a habit that you know that works against you, if it's overcoming self-destructive behavior, if it's retraining your thinking, if it's reinventing yourself, if it's trying to begin to design your relationship differently—all of us have a possibility by focusing and really harnessing our attention and concentrating on it. We really have the power available to us to honor our commitments in those particular areas.

Number one, make it a priority. No one would go get on an airplane if you thought your chances of getting to your destination were as good as your luggage. Am I correct? I say the reason that you will reach your destination more times than your luggage will is because the airline has made it a priority to move the human beings from one point to the other safely. I'm not really upset when my luggage doesn't show up. I'm glad they delivered me because they've made me a priority. They have made delivering you to your destination important. If you want to honor your commitment, whatever you decide that you're going to do, make sure you make it important. Make sure it is a priority.

Get started by finding one thing, one action step you can do towards your goal. Make sure it stretches you, that it challenges you, but it's doable—it has to be something that you can do. When I decided that I was going to exercise, I started out doing just ten sit-ups and ten push-ups. I knew I could do that. I started out small. Now, I'm up to fifty, but if I tried to do fifty starting out, I wouldn't be doing it. I started doing it in manageable segments. Do that, little by little, build on that, and it strengthens your will. My commitment now is strengthened and fortified by the activity of actually doing it. Now I can expand and build from there. When

I decided to begin to manage my money differently I started saving 5% of my money, then I increased it to 10%, then to 15%. Now I have disciplined myself to live off 75% of my income.

It took discipline to do that but I started watching how I was spending my money. I started keeping a log and following myself. You want to begin to find something that is manageable that you know that you can do.

The next tool in beginning to keep your commitments to yourself, is to have some friends that will hold you accountable. Friends that won't let you off the hook, that won't tolerate anything less than the best from you, people that will support you in this new way of being, in this new state of consciousness.

It is important to have a contingency plan. Many times, when you make a commitment to do something, there can be variables you can't control or you perhaps did not think about. You want to have some other plans going on. Most people don't keep their commitments because when something goes wrong, they just stop. They don't have a contingency plan. They don't know what to do next. As you challenge yourself you need to become creative and flexible.

Many times I say, "I don't know what to do." Then, I ask myself, "But if I did know what to do, what would it be?" That activates another part of my mind. Now start thinking about the possibilities and just experiment. Many of us just stop dead in our tracks. *I don't know what to do.* You do know what to do. You've got genius in you. Challenge yourself, push yourself, and make yourself come up with something. Use your imagination. What you will find is that you know more than you realize, that you're more creative and more resourceful than you realize.

The more you do it, the easier it will become. At first, it's going to be a struggle and after you get into a certain level of consciousness, you will ask yourself, "How is it that I didn't see this before?" At the level that I'm managing my business now, they say, "Consciousness is what we are." I literally look at myself and say, "How is it that I didn't do this before? Why is it that I couldn't see this before?" I didn't see it before because I didn't challenge myself. I didn't put myself out here. This is the reason that most of us go through life never discovering our true greatness. The uncommitted life isn't worth living, because it doesn't produce anything.

You only make things happen, your life only counts, you only make a difference when you are committed, when you make a commitment with your life. The people that make a commitment with their lives, the people that make a commitment to their customers, the people that make a commitment to their families, to their relationships, are the people that make the greatest impact in life.

What is commitment? Commitment is the sales-man who says, "Look here, I'm going to make $1,000 a day and I'm not going home until I do. You can turn the lights out. The janitors could be running the vacuum cleaner. I'm not leaving here until I do it." I used to be a door-to-door salesman, I had X number of TVs. I had a minimum amount that I knew I had to sell every day in order to provide for my mother who was ill at the time, who had lost her job because of arthritis. I said I'm going to go door to door.

Sometimes I would not come home until 1:00 a.m. I would be out knocking on doors.

"What do you want?"

"Would you like to buy a nice working television set, no money down?"

"No."

"What about an Emerson TV?"

"No."

"Thank you very much. Do you know anybody else that would be interested?"

"No."

"Thank you very kindly."

Knock on another. "Hello? Would you like to buy a nice, working television set, no money down?"

"No. Get away from our door."

"Thank you very kindly. Do you know anybody else would be?"

"Yeah, my cousin. He lives two doors down."

"Thank you very kindly. I'll tell him you sent me."

"Wanda, hey, your cousin told me that you want to buy a television set, told me to come here and talk to you. We got a special discount for you."

"Yes, come in. I'm interested."

I would just keep right on. I would not go home until I did it. It's an interesting thing, that when we put ourselves in a situation where we say we're going to do it, it puts you in another zone and the universe responds when you have that kind of consciousness.

The universe responds to the man or woman that refuses to be denied because that is your commitment. That business that you want, that book you want to write, that dream that you have of controlling your destiny—that is yours. That power to create that, to manifest that, that is yours. That's available to you, but you've got to be willing to stand there and face disappointment, to not have support, to be lonely, to doubt yourself sometimes, to be rejected again and again and again, to become bankrupt if necessary, again and again and again, and refuse to turn around until life gives it up. Nothing can resist a person who has that kind of commitment, these are the people that have made a difference on the planet.

John F. Kennedy said, "We will go to the moon in the next decade." He spoke it. That was a commitment and people shared that vision. People bought into that. We've had all kinds of examples in history where people have made declarations, who have committed their lives to bring about a difference. There are people who are taking a stand today against hunger. I guarantee you it will be a part of our past at some point in time. Someone took a stand against polio. It no longer plagues us as it once did because someone said, "It is my commitment to eradicate it from the face of the earth." Someone made the commitment. The reason that we're here and enjoying the democracy that we have, someone made a commitment that whatever is required—we will do it. I love what Paul Robeson said, "Here I stand for I can do no other," and that's how you must be.

Commitment means standing up for your life. It means honoring yourself. It means beginning to say, to see, and to recognize your alignment and oneness with the universe, and that you are a channel for life to express through. We short-circuit it with anger, we short-circuit it with fear, we short-circuit it with envy, we short-circuit it by being lazy, apathetic, or giving up easily. Why? We say, "Oh, it's too hard." We don't challenge our spirit. There is nothing as powerful as the human spirit. You can't destroy the human spirit. You can pervert it but you can't destroy it.

I'm reading *Man's Search for Meaning* by Viktor Frankl. What a powerful book. I'm reading it now for the seventh time. He gives so many graphic examples of the power of the human spirit. What are some of the things that can fortify us and give us the kind of inner strength that will allow us to propel ourselves into the future by manifesting our commitments?

In some cases, commitment means going back to school, getting some training, sitting up in classes with people younger than you, putting yourself in a position where you don't know, and that is awkward and uncomfortable. Yet because of your commitment to develop yourself or to go back to school, to get a high school diploma or to get a college degree, you decide it doesn't matter, you keep at it. Commitment can mean a lot of things. Sometimes it means you've got to back up. You might have to back up, to regroup and come back again because life has waylaid you, because you got knocked down.

When I was working on my dreams there were challenging times. I lost my house at one point. I lost my car, I was broke, my credit was bad, I was sleeping at different friends' houses on their couch or floor. There were times, months, that I slept on the floor of my office and got up early and dressed before my staff got there to give them the impression that I got there before they did. We all pretended not to know that the boss was staying in the office; we never talked about it.

I refused to give up on my dreams, and what happened? They say, "In the prosperous years, you put it in your pocket. In the lean years, you put it in your heart." It makes me appreciate it even more. I wouldn't trade for anything the disappointment and the pain that I have gone through by keeping the commitment.

Keeping the commitments that you have might mean taking a stand that's unpopular. Dr. King said, "Cowardice asks the question 'Is it safe?' Vanity asks the question 'Is it popular?' But conscience asks the question 'Is it right?'" Many people would rather operate from the first two. "Is it safe for me to take this position?" When I was a state legislator, I saw men and women who believed in legislation very strongly but when the Speaker of the House said, "We won't go with that," they backed down and felt bad about it. They wouldn't take the position because they didn't want the Speaker of the House to be angry with them. They wanted to be all right with all of the rest of their colleagues.

It takes a great deal of strength, courage, and commitment on your part to step out of line. Henry David Thoreau said, "If a man does not keep pace with his companions, perhaps it is because he hears a different drummer. Let him step to the music which he hears, however measured or far away." When you are committed, you are dancing to the beat of a different drummer. Don't expect people to understand you. Don't expect why you have to do this, why you have to go, why you leave, to make sense to anybody.

This is a good job. "I'm going." They pay you well. "I'm going." You're just a few years from retirement. "I'm going." Why? I don't understand. "You don't have to understand. I'm going for me because I've made a different kind of commitment with my life. This is something I have to do." Commitment means taking a stand, taking a stand for you. It means delivering. It means coming through.

What if you don't keep your commitment, Les? What if you give it everything you have and you come up short, or if you don't give it everything you have? What if you get weak along the way and you throw in the towel on yourself, you surrender to your emotions? What then? A lot of people become discouraged. They become frustrated. They say, "Oh, what the heck," and they go back to doing what they were doing before, saying it doesn't work.

Here's what I suggest. Number one, that does happen. Take total responsibility for it; just own it. Don't make any excuses why you gave in or why you didn't come through. Just own it and face the flack, whatever it is. Stand up inside yourself. Next thing is, assess the situation. How did you get here? What happened that you broke down, that you had a breakdown and you surrendered? What happened? What was going on? When I used to go on a diet—which I no longer do since I made a commitment to having a healthy lifestyle—I used to eat until 12:00 midnight on Sunday anything that wasn't moving. On Monday, I would get up and eat fruit, get a light breakfast. For lunchtime, I would fix some broiled chicken and meticulously peel the skin off, eat the chicken, and then eat the skin. Do five sit-ups, look in the mirror, and become discouraged because my stomach didn't look like a washboard or one of the Alvin Ailey dancers. I'd say, "What's the use?" and then go to refrigerator and eat cold food standing right there. When I evaluated where I broke down, I realized I can't have junk food in the house, so I had to remove that. Then I realized there are certain streets I couldn't drive down. I changed my route. I stopped taking people to lunch or to dinner because I couldn't sit there and watch them eat. When I had to go speak someplace where they were eating, I asked them to call me downstairs when it was time for me to speak, because if I sat at the table the food was going to call my name. I know this. I had to begin to make sure that I wasn't putting myself in a position where I would give up on my commitment.

I began to strategize how to avoid situations where I knew I could become weak. Another thing I do when I don't keep my commitment, I either deny myself something or I do a trade-off. If a glazed doughnut takes advantage of me, then I require myself to do an extra twenty-five sit-ups or I walk an extra fifteen or twenty minutes because I've got a hammerlock on my head that says, "Commit to that or do this." You might have to deny yourself something or do a trade-off, but find something that will offset it.

Then, start again. So what if you fell flat on your face? So what? Start again. Learn from experience and start again. Don't count yourself out. Don't sentence yourself to a lifetime of being miserable, a lifetime of being broke, a lifetime of being unhealthy, a lifetime of being in a relationship that is no longer fulfilling to you, a lifetime of working on a job that does not bring you satisfaction or that's not giving you the creative juice that you need.

You don't have to sentence yourself like that. You are a human being. Don't discount your life that way. Your life has too much value to the universe. You've got something to contribute. You've got something to give. So what if you make a commitment and you're not able to do it like a pro, that you're not good as everybody else? Live in the moment.

I like this ancient Sanskrit poem, "Look to this day for it is life, the very life of life. In its brief course lie all the realities and verities of existence, the bliss of growth, the splendor of action, the glory of power, for yesterday is but a dream and tomorrow is only a vision. Today well-lived makes every yesterday a dream of happiness and every tomorrow a vision of hope. Look well, therefore, to this day."

We can make that kind of commitment to enjoy where we are, to feel the experience of life where we are, to do all we can right now where we are. Forget about the mistakes of yesterday; forget about all your failures yesterday, forget about what you don't have. That's not important. The only thing that we have is right now and I say that life is good, calling on you to call forth on that.

I think one of the most positive groups in the world is Optimists International, and I want to share *The Optimist Creed* by Christian Larson. It is also known as "Promise yourself," which for our purposes here I changed to, "Commit yourself" because I think that commitment has the power we are talking about here.

Commit yourself . . .
To be so strong that nothing can disturb your peace of mind.
To talk health, happiness, and prosperity to every person you meet.
To make all your friends feel that there is something in them.

To look at the sunny side of everything and make your optimism come true.

To think only of the best, to work only for the best and expect only the best.

To be just as enthusiastic about the success of others as you are about your own.

To forget the mistakes of the past and press on to the greater achievements of the future.

To wear a cheerful countenance at all times and give every living creature you meet a smile.

To give so much time to the improvement of yourself that you have no time to criticize others.

To be too large for worry, too noble for anger, too strong for fear, and too happy to permit the presence of trouble.

Commit yourself to these things.

Isn't that powerful? What a commitment to make with your life. Commit yourself to stretch, to get outside of your comfort zone and not be concerned about what people think about you because they're thinking it anyhow. Don't worry about what they will say. They're already saying it. Why do you care? Decide that your life has so much meaning to the planet. Decide that you have something to give. That's why you're here. You didn't just show up. You brought something here.

You're in a journey, you have a destination, a mission to achieve, to do, to implement, to perform, to experience. Decide to commit yourself to be an adventurer in life. Look out on life around you. Look within yourself and say, "Where is it in my life that I need to make a commitment right now?" It might be for your health. It might be to be a happier person. It might be to make a difference in your community. It might be that. Where is it?

I say that commitment shows up and the man or woman rises up, the ones who have some idea, some dream that they've been nurturing within themselves and no one believed it. No one thought for them, but they weren't masters at it, they weren't experts at it. No one would build them a statue and call their name and recognize them. They never made it to the front page of the newspaper but they had something that was there, something that was their baby, something that they loved and they believed in, and they just did what they could with what God gave them with their dream.

Commitment shows up and people that are willing to give themselves a chance, who look at their lives, will look within themselves, and say, "I know that this just cannot be it for my life. I know that there's something I'm supposed to do. I don't know right now." Maybe you do know and you've talked yourself out of it. I understand that because I'm a late bloomer. But then I say, no, no, no. Everything happens as it should. I got the courage to step out, to become committed. I was seriously not serious, until I decided. It took me some time to build up the courage, to become committed, because it frightened me.

I wish I could tell you I've been doing this for my whole life. I haven't, but I am doing it now. I'm just glad I decided to become committed before I left here. Wherever you are, decide that you're going to commit your life now. Now! Let it show up in your contribution. Let it show up in what you have to share. Whatever commitment that you make, honor that commitment as yourself, honor your word as yourself. Whatever you put out there, do it with all that you have, with all your consciousness, with all your commitment.

CHAPTER 14

The Power of Self-Fulfillment

We've been going through several stages of personal growth. We looked at self-awareness, asking that central question "Who am I?" and looking at your strengths and your weaknesses, getting some evaluation, determining what it is you want out of life. Then we examined self-approval, allowing yourself to do the things that you'd like to do, and going after the dreams that you'd like to go after. We know when we don't approve of our dreams because of the ways we can avoid working towards them. We don't act on them. We procrastinate. We come up with a variety of excuses on why we're not going into action.

Now we arrive at self-commitment, which finds us going for that dream, going for those goals, deciding to do the things that are necessary to bring about the changes that we want in our lives or in society. When you are involved in commitment—when you are implementing your plan of action—you're going to produce some results. You're going to have some victories that you can feel good about and it's a time of celebration.

What happens when you reach the level of self-fulfillment? First of all, we can acknowledge that self-fulfillment is unending and should be viewed in that context. Robert Schuller says it best, "Success is never-ending." That means that we never get to a level where we feel there's nothing else for us to do, that we've achieved a certain number of goals and we figure that we are through. No. You don't want to stay there and celebrate too long like a lot of people do. They do something they consider outstanding. They go around talking about what they used to do. Let me tell you I used to do this and I used to do that.

Excuse me; but as the saying goes, used-to-be's don't make no honey. What are you doing now? What have you done lately? Going around telling people what you used to do and who you used to be, what does that count for now? What are you doing *now*? You're still here breathing. That means you've got some more to give. It doesn't matter how old you are, it doesn't matter where you are, it doesn't matter what you have, it doesn't matter what you've done.

Life is about growing, it's about being productive, it's about stretching, and it's about challenging yourself. You start looking around and decide what else do I want to do? What got me here? It's a time for celebration, but also a time for reflection. What got me here? What worked? What did not work? What do I need to repeat so that I can get the same kind of results in other areas of my life? If the goal is to improve my health, if the goal is to improve my relationship, if the goal is to improve my income, if the goal is to improve something in society, what is it I need to do?

Don't confuse *what you do* with *who you are*. Don't go on some type of ego trip by talking about all you've done. None of us do anything by ourselves. Develop an appreciation for external support as well as good fortune because those things play a role. Don't go overboard celebrating. Rudyard Kipling said, "You must meet with triumph and disaster and treat those two impostors just the same."

Look at it and say, "Hey, I did it. I feel good about that." Now you're moving on to the next thing. Or, perhaps things did not work out the way you wanted them to. You didn't produce the results you wanted. "Okay, I missed that." You win some, you lose some and now you're moving right along. Don't confuse who you are with what you do.

You return to the area of self-assessment and start looking at yourself and evaluating yourself *now*. What are some of the elements, characteristics and qualities of people who are fulfilled, who live a life of fulfillment? What are some of the things we can look at with them?

Number one, make your mind fertile ground for the seeds of opportunity. If you want to experience a sense of fulfillment, you must have an open mind, so that ideas can come in there and take root and grow. Part of beginning to have fertile ground is that you have to break that ground up. Break up that hard crust because if you don't, seeds will fall there and the wind can blow them away—the winds of doubt. When you're setting your mind and you refuse to grow and you're not open to new ideas, new methods, new ways of doing things, if your mind is already fixed, you become stagnant. You can't grow. You can't have a sense of fulfillment. You become extremely cynical and negative about everything. You know it all.

Learn to look at life and have a sense of curiosity, don't be a know-it-all. You want to keep learning and growing. Here's what I see as our theme, "You never find out how much you know until you find out how little you know." There are some people you can't tell anything. They have all the answers. "Oh, I've already done that."

A friend relayed this observation from a flight he took. Two men were sitting together. One was finished reading a magazine and said to the other, "Would you like to read this magazine? I'm finished and want to share it with you" "No, I read that before. Don't like it." Okay. "What about this *USA Today*?" "No, I read that before. I don't like that either." After the food was served the first man notice his companion wasn't eating and asked, "Would you care to have anything I have here?" "No. I tried that before. I don't like that." Next, we can presume he only has one child!

This story illustrates how often we can go through life prejudging things. Let's look at buttermilk. How many of us like it? But how many have actually tasted it? If I just don't like the way it looks. I might be missing out on something. Many of us count ourselves out of things prematurely. Without examining, you just don't know what the possibilities are.

You want to be open, you want to continue to learn, you want to continue to grow, you want to begin to know that there are unlimited ideas out here waiting for you to discover. If you don't take advantage of them when they come your way because you're so close-minded, understand that somebody else will. We've all had ideas that we did not act on and then somebody else had the idea and went with it. Learn to be curious, open and receptive.

The next thing in living a fulfilling life is to become involved in life. Live your fantasy. Most people go through life not living their fantasy, sitting up in the bleachers, looking out onto the field, wishing they were down there, just fantasizing. I used to do that. I used to imagine myself at a basketball game. "One second to go, Les Brown comes down court. He looks to his right, looks to his left. He's the only one that can do it. Swoosh, the ball goes in. Les saved us," and people picked me up and carried me off. I never went out and did it.

Decide to live your fantasy. You can go through life, you can come up with reasons or you can come up with results. You can come up with excuses or you can come up with achievements. You can go through life blaming or you can come up with solutions. The choice is in your hands—satisfaction or despair. We can choose that.

Look at your life and decide what it is that you want to do that will give it a sense of worth. Someone said that your life worth is measured by your accomplishments and not by your complaints. Want to have a fulfilling life? Decide not to make your life predictable. Sometimes our lives can be too predictable—a little too routine, day in and day out. You don't always get much juice out of a life like that. What happens if we change it up? Variety most certainly is the spice of life.

Here's another way to create a greater sense of ful-fillment? Challenge your fears. Look those fears in the face and take them on. Don't allow them to rule you. Decide that you're going to take some chances.

One day My friend Adrian decided to have a day of challenge, so he and a friend went to the amuse-ment park. He's always been afraid of certain rides, so he said on this particular day, he decided that he was going to go on the most dangerous rides.

They went around looking at all the rides. His friend said, "That's the one there. That's it." He said, "Why that one?" She said, "Well, I read about it in the newspaper. Two people were killed last year on that." He said, "Yes, that's the one I want. That's the one." He got in the long line. After nearly two hours waiting in line, as they started getting closer, he started doubting himself. "Maybe I shouldn't do this."

His friend insisted, "Get back in line." He said, "No, no, no. I changed my mind. I don't want to do this. I don't have to do the most dangerous ride." He started visual-izing himself being thrown out of this big ride and his name on the front page of the newspaper. He just started saying, "No, I don't want to do it," but she insisted. "Come on, Adrian. We said we're going to do it. We're going to confront our fears today. Come on, just stay in line."

He kept arguing with her the whole time. They got to the front of the line and the attendant called,

"Okay. Next." He said, "No. I just decided to change my mind." She said, "Come on," and pushed him on. They strapped him in. As they begin to move, he said, "Wait a minute. I want to get out," but it was too late. "Oh, no. Please, please I got a bad heart. Let me out."

He screamed all throughout that ride, his friend was laughing. A wig came off. He lost his hat. Adrian says, "Les, when I got off that ride, I walked a little taller." He said he felt good inside. "It wasn't that bad after all." We've all experienced things that we dreaded doing. When we finally did it, we say, "Hey, it wasn't as bad as I thought it was going to be."

That's what many people miss out on in life. You've got to be willing to risk. If you're not willing to risk, you can't grow. Life has no power when you're not willing to risk. Here is an inspirational poem by William Arthur Ward called "To Risk."

To laugh is to risk appearing the fool,
To weep is to risk appearing sentimental.

To reach out for another is to risk involvement,
To expose feelings is to risk exposing your true self.

To place your ideas and dreams
before a crowd is to risk their loss.

To love is to risk not being loved in return.
To hope is to risk despair.
To try is to risk failure.

But risks must be taken because the greatest
  hazard in life is to risk nothing.

The person who risks nothing, does nothing, has
  nothing, is nothing.

He may avoid suffering and sorrow
But he cannot learn, feel, change, grow or live.

Chained by his servitude he is a slave who has
  forfeited all freedom.

Only a person who risks is free.

I'm reminded of a story about a missionary who had gone to Africa to work with a tribe called the Head-hunters. There was a reporter observing them and for a long period of time, the missionary had a limited relationship with the tribe. They would not take him in. He was tentative, hesitant, and fearful, and he didn't want to risk having a relationship with them because he didn't want to mess around and have his head taken off. He had this fear and obviously, it showed and the tribesman sensed it.

Finally the reporter returned and saw he had developed an incredible relationship with the tribesman, these Headhunters. He asked the missionary, "What happened? How did you convert the distance, the hostility into a warm, close relationship?" He replied, "I had a dream one night. I was asking what my passion is, what's my life goal? I always wanted to be a missionary. This is the work I love."

In the dream he asked himself, "How much do you love it?" I said, "I'm willing to die for this dream." When he woke up, he said he acknowledged that this was, in fact, his passion, that it was, in fact, his life's work, and that he loved doing this so much that he was willing to die for it. Therefore, he no longer had any fear of death. He said, "When you no longer fear dying, what else can life threaten you with? What else?"

Here's a view of commitment which I love. The next time you have bacon and eggs, look at it. The chicken was involved, but the pig was committed. He had to give it all up. When you're willing to give it all up—that's what life is. You got to be willing to give it all up. When you're willing to throw it all on the line, that's when life takes on a whole new dimension. Most people won't do that. They won't risk that. Decide to take some risks.

You want to break the routine. Most people go through life following that routine and we know that that is a living death. Going through life, playing it safe is like a breathing corpse, because the only way to grow is to risk. The only way that you can become your best is to risk. You have to challenge yourself. You have to venture into the unknown and take some chances, put yourself on the line. As you get out of your comfort zone, you expand your whole life and open yourself up to gaining a sense of fulfillment.

The more you do, the more you realize you can do. You expand your capacity, you expand your potential, you expand your horizons, and you expand your vision of yourself and of life. You expand your participation in life. You're more involved in life. You'll get more out of life because you're putting more into life. That's why it's so important that we are willing to take some risks.

"I don't know exactly what to do." It's okay. You'll find out. You either learn that you're going in the right direction or the wrong direction. You'll get some feedback. The universe will tell you. "Where do I get started?" Just get started. The universe will give you immediate feedback. Don't worry. If you hit your head long enough, you'll get the message. Lose enough money, you'll learn quickly. Get enough knots on your head. It will be all right.

Here's something else. Choose to be happy in spite of life's challenges. Life changes every day. Sometimes things will be going your way. Sometimes things work well for you. Sometimes it won't work so well. Sometimes you have your health, you're feeling good and energetic, and you have a yes-I-can attitude. All of that can go. There are some things that can happen to us in life that can take all of that away. Illness, accidents, financial crisis—life is always changing, and you can choose in the midst of it to be happy in spite of it. In the good times and the bad, you can make a choice. In *Man's Search for Ultimate Meaning*, Viktor Frankl said, "The last of the human freedoms: to choose one's attitude in any given set of circumstances, to choose one's own way."

Douglas Malloch has a poem I love, entitled, "It's Fine Today."

Sure, this world is full of trouble.
    I ain't say it ain't.
Lord, I've had enough and double
    Reason for complaint;
Rain and storm have come to fret me,
    Skies are often gray;
Thorns and brambles have beset me
    On the road—but say,
    Ain't it fine today?

What's the use of always weepin',
     Making trouble last?
What's the use of always keepin'
     Thinkin' of the past?
Each must have his tribulation—
     Water with his wine;
Life, it ain't no celebration,
     Trouble?—I've had mine—
     But today is fine!

It's today that I am livin',
     Not a month ago.
Havin'; losin'; takin'; givin';
     As time wills it so.
Yesterday a cloud of sorrow
     Fell across the way,
It may rain again tomorrow,
     It may rain—but say,
     Ain't it fine today?"

I like that. Even if a cloud of sorrow comes over here, isn't it fine today—living in the moment, getting everything we can out of where we are, right now, living in the present.

Another important factor is the willingness to let people and things go. You want to live a life of fulfillment. You've got to be willing to let certain people go in your life, especially if they want to go. Don't get addicted to material things. Be willing to let things or people go. When they're no longer good for you, just let them go. Holding on tenaciously just to hold on really doesn't make sense. Sometimes we're just holding on because we don't realize we don't need it, we might desire it but we really don't need it.

It's important to face the truth about life and death and deal with it. Often, when someone we love very much dies, we allow that loss to take such a toll we can make ourselves miserable. Some literally will themselves to die early because they feel lost without this person; they have nothing to look forward to. Life has other opportunities, other relationships, other experiences for us, and the people that we love really want us to go on.

It's good to remember that things are always going to happen to us. In order to have a fulfilling life, know that things are going to happen—you must expect the unexpected. Whatever happens to you, use everything for your upliftment, learning, and growth. Everything that happens, use it for your upliftment. Learn and grow in the midst of it. Ask, "What can I learn from this? What can I get from this? How did I end up here? What's the blessing in this for me?" Ask yourself that whatever it is and don't let it go until you get your blessing out of it because there's a blessing there, there's a lesson there, there's something for you in everything that happens to you, for you to learn from that experience. Look at it, examine it, analyze it, dissect it, take it apart until it reveals itself to you. Then get what you need from that experience and move on from everything that happens to you.

I have a friend who stutters and I asked her if she was taking any special classes to stop from stuttering. She said she wasn't because it helps her business. She continued, "When I go to somebody, I say, 'Now, if you're busy, I'll come back because I stutter,' and they used to say, 'Oh no. You can tell me right now.' Then I delivers my sales pitch and after I goes through it if they say no, I say, 'Well, you didn't understand. Let me tell you again.' They then say, 'Oh no. That's all right. How much did you say it is? That's all right. Don't tell me any more. Just let me know how much I need to give you so you can get out of here.'" She's turned that stuttering to her advantage. Somebody said, "If life gives you a lemon, write yourself a lemon cookbook."

I have people say to me, "Hey, I really feel sorry for you. It's a shame they labeled you 'educable mentally retarded.'" I said, "It's okay." I've told this story before workshops at AT&T, Procter and Gamble, McDonald's Corporations, Xerox. Whatever happens to you, turn it to your advantage. I have now determined that it is a blessing for me as opposed to a handicap. I would eventually prove those labels wrong by engaging in self-study and consciously working to develop myself. Now they have to ask themselves what they were thinking about when they used those labels for me? What was going on?

Here is something I encourage you to do. Whatever you do, do it in a consciousness of love. If you love what you do, and if you decide to love people, to make wherever you are an experience of love, just decide to be a loving person regardless if the people you're around are loving or not. I've never read anywhere where they say, "God has love." I never read that. How does it go? It's "God is love," not "God has love." If we are the children of God, we are the offspring of God, then we are what? Love. Love is not an emotion. Love is not something you can give. You can't give love. You must be love. You've got to be a loving person. As you learn to operate in that consciousness remember this does not just come to us overnight or just someone recommending it. Enlightenment, insight, come to us only with practice—practice, practice and more practice. We gain insight by doing it and doing it and doing it some more. It takes a lot of working consciously.

Emmet Fox said, "Love is absolutely invincible," and went on to describe it in a poem simply called "Love."

There is no difficulty that enough love
will not conquer; No disease that enough love
will not heal, No door that enough love
will not open; No gulf that enough love
will not bridge; No wall that enough love
will not throw down; No sin that enough love
will not redeem.

It makes no difference how deeply
seated may be the trouble, How
hopeless the outlook, How muddled the
tangle, How great the mistake; A
sufficient realization of love will dissolve
it all. If only you could love enough
you would be the happiest and most
powerful being in the world.

He goes on to quote a scripture that says, "God is love, and he that dwelleth in love, dwelleth in God, and God in him." Decide to be a loving experience in life. Whatever work you have to do, do it lovingly. Whatever relationships that you have, just decide to be more loving, more giving, more caring, more concerned, more sensitive than you've ever been before.

What if you don't get it back? It would be great if you get it back, but don't count on it. You might get it back and you might not. Don't let someone else determine who you're going to be. Be who you are. Give what you want. Why? Because you want it back? No, do it because that's who you are. Do it because that's how you have decided to live your life. Do it because it gives your life a sense of fulfillment, worth, and self-respect. When we get off-center, when we allow people or circumstances to determine whether or not we are loving because of the way they treat us or because of what we are experiencing, then we are not controlling our destiny, we're not determining what happens *to* us and *for* us. That's the power that we have been given, the power to choose yes.

Ask yourself, right now, who do you serve? Do you serve those negative feelings and emotions? Anybody can hate, anybody can be revengeful. Some people would rather get revenge than get ahead in life. Anybody can do that. Anybody can hold a grudge. It doesn't take any greatness for that. We don't need any motivation or encouragement to hold a grudge. What good does it do to hold resentment or bitterness in your heart? The real challenge is about growth and moving into your greatness and about being who you are, being true to you.

I like what Charles Fillmore said at age ninety-four, "I fairly sizzle with zeal and enthusiasm as I spring forth with a mighty faith to do the things that ought to be done by me." As you go toward your goals and your dreams, spring forth with a mighty faith to write the book that ought to be written by you, to sing the song that ought to be sung by you, to start the business that ought to be started by you, to help the people that ought to be helped by you, and to make the difference in our society that ought to be made by you.

Determine what your life work is. Ask yourself: What is the work that I ought to do? How is it that I can make my life a great experiment? How is it that I can make the contribution that I showed up to give, something that when I go to sleep at night, I can feel good within myself and know that I've given life my very best.

One last step in striving toward self-fulfillment is gratitude. It is important to live in a spirit and an attitude of gratitude. There are so many things that we take for granted. There are so many things that we need to be thankful for. There are big things, there are little things. I'm thankful for my health, I'm thankful for my children, I'm thankful for my mother, I'm thankful for you, I'm thankful for the life that I live and for the people who have enriched my life, who have contributed to my being who I am.

Sometimes, just lying there in the middle of the night, staring at the ceiling, I just say, "Thank you, Lord." When I look back on my life, I've come a mighty long way. Even if I don't reach my goals, I'm thankful for this journey. Thank you very much. Thank you.

CHAPTER 15

The Power of Motivation

I define motivation as "the desire to achieve that which you believe to be worthwhile." In this chapter we will look at some keys to self-motivation. Many people go through life never getting in touch with their greatness because they lack the motivation to push themselves or simply because they have not found anything they believe to be worthwhile enough to challenge them. There is a line from Thomas Gray's Elegy *Written in a Country Churchyard*, "Many a flower has bloomed unceasingly and wasted sweetness upon the cold desert air." To me this simply means that many talented persons have gone unnoticed and the world never had a chance to be exposed to their talent because that person did not take the time to express, demonstrate or motivate themselves toward bringing forward that which they came into the universe to bring.

How can you measure your motivation? How can you evaluate where you are on a scale of 1 to 10? Let's do this for ourselves mentally. How do you rate yourself from 1 to 10, your mental attitude about yourself, how you feel about you, how you feel about life? How do you rate yourself on a scale of 1 to 10 in terms of your physical appearance, in terms of your health? Do you take care of yourself? Are you allowing yourself to get overweight and out of shape? Are you conscious of your health? Are you watching the food that you take into your body? Do you make a deliberate effort to exercise? George Burns said, "We cannot help getting older but we don't have to get old." Many of us get old before our time because we don't take time to take care of ourselves.

Your environment is a very good indicator. On a scale of 1 to 10, is it what you want it to be? Do you find it desirable? Are you satisfied with the job or career that you're involved in? Eighty-five percent of Americans are unhappy with their jobs. Are you spending eight hours a day just doing time? Are you doing something that you don't find challenging, that does not make you stretch mentally, that does not stimulate you, that does not inspire you? Do you find any sense of fulfillment in it? If you're doing that day in and day out, it has to affect how you feel about yourself, and your level of motivation.

Look at your relationships. What kind of impact are they having on your life? Are they nourishing or toxic? Do they drain you or build you up? Ask yourself that. How motivated are you to do something about it?

What are your contributions, your actions; what are you giving? Many people will leave the universe without a trace. Will anybody know that you came this way? What contribution are you giving? What will you leave? What will be different because you came this way?

I like the expression that says our life is a gift that God has given us and how we live our lives is our gift to God. What kind of gift are you formulating? Is this a gift that you'd like to take back and do something else with before you turn it in? Think about that. What can we do? What are some of the keys that we can begin to use to motivate ourselves when our batteries run low? I don't care who you are or what you do. At some time, you are going to get tired, you're going to get in a rut. It might seem like nothing you do works out and you just don't have the wherewithal or the will to do anything. You're just wading through life, just doing time, day in and day out, looking at non-discriminatory television, anything that's on, just looking.

Depressed. Feeling powerless. Feeling useless and bored. What do you do? How do you get yourself out of a rut? When you know you can do more than what you've been doing and you're not doing it, when you're discontented with where you are and you get angry at yourself, how do you motivate yourself?

One of the things we can do is to stay involved in self-mastery. You must work on yourself continuously. Never be satisfied with yourself. As you invest the effort and time on yourself, know that it's the greatest ability that human beings have over animals. A dog can't be anything but a dog. A tree can't be anything but a tree. As a human being, you've got unlimited potential. You can put effort into you, and by concentrating on you, and developing you, you can transform your life right now.

There are so many ways you can work on yourself. You can read books that inspire and motivate you. You can listen to recordings and podcasts over and over and over again. I suggest you listen to them when you first get up in the morning. You want to control the spirit of your day. When you first wake up in the morning, your mind is operating at 10.5 wave cycles per second. That's when the subconscious mind is most impressionable. Whatever you hear in the first twenty minutes after you wake up, that will affect the spirit of your day. When you listen to them, listen with relaxed belief, believing that this can happen for you. Listen to them over and over and over again, and you will get a breakthrough. You can listen to the same one for months, and all of a sudden, you'll hear something you've never heard before, and it will have a special meaning for you. When you read the same book over again and you might find some special insight. You'll say, "I can't believe I didn't see that the first time."

Get involved in developing yourself. Most people won't do that. Most people won't take that kind of effort and invest that kind of energy in themselves because they fall prey to that conversation within. "Oh, don't do that. You don't have time. You're too busy. You're too caught up in the rat race." Most people won't do that. They won't take time to go to lectures or seminars. They won't take time to go to classes to improve themselves.

As you continue to work on yourself, you will begin to expand your vision of yourself. You will begin to work towards self-mastery and you will begin to see it reflect itself in all the dimensions of your life, your mental life, your physical life, your social life, in your relationships, your monetary life. Concentrate on developing yourself because if you don't, I guarantee you that you will make a settlement, and most people have, and most of us already have. What kind of settlement have you made with your life? When we make settlements out of court that usually means you've decided to take something less than what you originally wanted to get had you gone into court. And the reason that you settled outside of court is because you didn't believe that you can get it, so you made an out-of-court settlement. Many of us are making in-life settlements. We're settling for less than what we actually deserve. We don't feel good about it, but we make it work in our minds. We come up with some kind of excuse to make it all right. What kind of settlement have you made with your life?

Many of us settle for less than what we want out of relationships because we don't have the courage to change them. I used to run a seminar called *Are You Living Together or Dying Together?* Many people are just dying together. As Gladys Knight sang "neither one of us wants to be the first to say goodbye."

As you work on yourself, you feel good about yourself, and as you feel better about yourself, you'll treat yourself differently. Now the next thing is to develop a health plan. You can't feel well and do well if you don't have good health. You can't perform if you don't have your health. Your health is valuable. Develop a health plan, a plan that you will follow because this body is the only vehicle you have to carry you through this experience called life.

You want to take good care of it because you love you enough. You care enough about you and that's not easy. It is not easy having a health plan and sticking to it, but you're worth it, doing it again and again and again. I have lost twenty-two pounds several times. I always do it. I love potato chips. People who know me know I love peanut M&Ms. I love peanut butter and jelly sandwiches. I love my mother's sweet potato pie. It's not always on my health plan but I put it there sometimes as I say, "Life is too short to go without sweet potato pie."

As you take care of yourself you can start to live life with energy and passion. You can make a conscious effort to be lively. You can smile. You can feel happy. We've got a lot to be thankful for but watch some of the faces around you every day, and observe that not all are good for us—depressed, angry, unhappy—so we learn to avoid these kinds of faces.

The next thing we can do is to monitor our inner conversations. Watch the things that you say to yourself, and then learn to take charge. A friend came one of my workshops and put this perfectly, "I didn't want to come tonight. I don't really feel like it. I'm feeling so depressed and then I said I'm going anyhow." You see, that was a conversation. We have them all the time so let's learn to watch what we say to ourselves. "Oh, you don't need to worry about trying to go into your own business. Forget that, you can't do that. What if you lose everything you've got?" "Les, don't do that. How can you possibly think about being a motivational speaker? You don't have the contacts, you don't have the money, you don't know the right people, and you're going to get up there and your mind's going to go blank." "Just forget all that. You remember that time you got up before some people and you panicked? You stood up in your mind, sat down? Don't you remember?" And then I finally said, "Shut up. I'm going to do it anyway." You've got to learn to stand up to yourself inside yourself, and override that conversation that's always going on. Eighty-five percent of what that conversation will tell you is negative. It will tell you you're tired when you really are not tired. It will tell you, you can't do it. It will fill you with fear, so you've got to watch that conversation, and when you find it going on, you've got to stand up to it and say, "I'm going to do this anyhow. I'm afraid but I'm afraid not to do it, and I'm not going to let you stop me." The biggest challenge that you will have in life is yourself. There's an old African proverb that says, "When there is no enemy within, the enemy outside can do us no harm."

The next key to self-motivation is to ask yourself, "What do I want out of life?" What do you want out of life? What do you want out of a job? What do you want out of a career? What do you want out of a relationship? What do you want? What gives you your life?

How will you know when you've got it? What will make you happy? You need to know. You need to start asking yourself some questions. What do I really, truly want? You need to be exact about that. Don't be vague. "Oh, I just want to be happy." That's too vague. What will make you happy? How will you know when you have gotten it?

Zero in on it. Be exact, be specific. As you do that, you will stimulate the subconscious mind to look for and find those things in your world. Once you begin to determine what you want, take the time to write it down. Don't just think about it, write it down. This is a subjective process that engages the subconscious mind. Write it down. Once you write it down, read it three times a day—morning, noon, and night.

Why is this important? Writing it down and repeating it will affect your focus. It will cause you to concentrate. When that other conversation is going on, telling you what you cannot do, telling you all of the impossibilities and all of the obstacles, your concentrating will begin to create a larger vision within yourself, and you'll start looking for and seeing some new opportunities. You'll start creating some openings for yourself. Saying your goals every day, day in and day out, will focus you. That will discipline your thinking, and you'll get all kinds of creative ideas. You're going to feel your adrenaline flowing, and you're going to think about some idea you had. You'll say, "I want to go back and I'm going to look at that again from a different vantage point, not from the level of the problem or the obstacles that I encountered, but from a higher vantage point." As you talk to the higher consciousness within you, you will begin to see and know that you are powerful; you are a miracle worker. That other inner conversation has conditioned you to believe that you're enough. You'll begin to discover the truth of who you are and be ready to face whatever challenges with the knowledge that you are powerful and that you're a miracle maker. And it starts with writing down exactly what it is that you want and reading it every day.

The next thing is to see yourself there. How will you feel once you get there? What will the experience be like for you? What will be different? What kind of person do you have to become in order to get there? Visualize yourself there, living the experience. I remember when I ran for state representative in Ohio I had a lot of people telling me, "Les, you can't possibly win. You can't do that." You not only have to watch out for the conversations within but also the ones outside.

So I went down to the legislature building and I saw myself. I knew what I wanted. I saw myself in the chair. I pointed out the chair that I wanted. I would sit up in the galleries and watch the legislative process. I attended the committee meetings and listened to legislation being introduced. I learned how to write legislation, and how to amend legislation. I started thinking like a legislator. I began to get up every day and dress and think like a legislator. I would see myself driving there, being there. "Mr. Speaker, I'm the gentleman from the 29th House District. I'd like to introduce a bill."

When I ran and won against overwhelming odds, they were shocked. To me it seemed I had won the election even before it was held because I was living it in my mind. You want to see yourself beyond your circumstances, beyond your challenges. See yourself with the challenge already resolved and knowing that all is well. See yourself in control and in charge of your destiny, being healthy and happy.

The next thing is extremely important for self-motivation; it's very important to know why you're doing it because your mind will say, "Why bother? Why go through all this? This is too hard. Throw in the towel. It's not worth it." Has your mind ever said that to you before? Here's how you can handle that and over-ride it. Write down five reasons why you deserve it. Why do you deserve what you want? Why you? What meaning and value will it bring to your life? What's so different about you that you deserve to reach this goal?

When you write down those five reasons, you can pull them out when you have down moments. When those conversations start both in your head and from the outside world—and they will start—you can read those reasons and they will build you up. They will be your rod and your staff to comfort you through challenging moments. Life will knock you between the eyes. It will catch you on the blindside, come out of nowhere. Stuff you can't anticipate will knock the wind out of you. You'll want to give up. That's why it's important to work on yourself, learning, building yourself up, talking to yourself with power, feeling, and conviction.

I want to share one of my experiences being blindsided. All was moving forward spectacularly as I was pursuing my dream. I had just given a great presentation, with 5,000 folks attending. After I finished and got a rousing standing ovation, I called the woman I was dating at the time. "Hey, guess what." I said, "They loved me. I got a standing ovation."

The audience was still chanting, "We want the motivator. We want the motivator."

I said, "Listen. Do you hear?"

She said, "Yes. Les, I need to talk to you."

"Wait a minute. I'll be home soon."

"Les, we need to talk."

I heard a voice in the background say, "Hurry up and tell him."

"Who's that?"

"Les, you've been gone a lot and there's somebody else."

"What?"

The organizers came in, "Come on, Mr. Motivator. They want you back out there."

"Wait a minute. Hold on. What did you say?"

"I'm sorry. There's someone else," and I heard a voice say, "Hang up the phone now." Click.

I said, "Wait a minute."

Again, "Hey, motivator. Come on. They want you. Can't you hear them cheer?"

I said, "Uh. Uh. Uh. Okay." I returned to the stage and started talking again. "When you're working on a larger vision, you've really got to work on yourself because life will catch you on the blindside," and then, "Make sure you really want it. You better be ready because sometimes it'll make you cry." Somebody said, "The spirit is on him." I was on fire, and talked until I was blinking in the lights and they had to take me off the stage. "Come on, Mr. Brown, it's time to go home." I went back to my hotel room, and loneliness and heartbreak were sitting on the bed, said, "Do you have your larger vision now? How's your positive attitude?"

Life will wear you out. You'll be saying, "No, I can't" and "No, I won't." You try to read it, but can't see through the tears. I went climbing through the drawers in this hotel, trying to find a Bible. "Somebody, anybody, help me. Yahweh, yahoo, anybody." That's why you have to work on yourself because life will send you some curves you cannot anticipate and you want to be ready.

Whatever you do, you want to develop technical mastery. You want to be the best at what you do. You want to master it. Part of self-motivation is finding something that gives you a strong sense of competence. When you become known for that, you develop a reputation of being good at doing that. You set some high personal standards for yourself. You're not competing with anybody else. You're just unfolding yourself to be the best person that you can be, to give the best quality service that you can give because that is a statement about who you are.

Another key to self-motivation is to recognize that you're going to get into some slumps, you're going to encounter a great deal of failure in life. It goes with the territory, but in the face of that, you want to be relentless. When you want something, don't expect everybody to say, "Come on in. You want this? Great. We want to give it to you. You're such a nice person." No. Life isn't like that. Many doors will be closed in your face. Many loan applications will come back with, "No. You don't have enough collateral. You don't have enough credit." It would be easy to give up, but you're going to shout back, "I'm going to be fearless. I refuse to be denied and I'm going to go all out. I'm going to be relentless. I don't care how many no's I encounter."

When Isaiah Thomas is getting ready for a basketball game he says, "I'm going to either shoot us in, or shoot us out, but I'm *not* going to *not do* anything." That's the way to go. You can't make a basket unless you shoot the ball. You can't hit a home run unless you take a swing at it. Most people won't even take a swing. "Well, I probably won't make it anyhow." That's the conversation within. "They probably won't give it to me anyhow." If you want something, you've got to be relentless. You've got to decide, "I deserve this and I'm going to have it," and you go all out to get it. That drives you.

When you want something out of life, you've got to be willing to go into action. Don't wait around for things to be just right. Don't wait for things to be perfect. Don't wait for the ideal situation. It will never be ideal. There will always be a reason. "Well, as soon as the children grow up," or "As soon as I pay my bills," or "As soon as I get my divorce," of "As soon as I get enough money together." Do what you can, where you are, with what you have, and never be satisfied. A lot of people never take a chance in life. They don't want to take any chances. That's not walking by faith. That's walking by sight. If I can see it, I'll do it. No, no, no. Some people say, "If I could see it, I'll believe it." No, no, no. If you believe it, you can see it. Don't be disturbed because no one else can see it. That's not unusual. That is ordinary but because you want some different kind of results in your life, you've got to be willing to be unreasonable.

If you want unreasonable results in your life, you've got to be willing to be unreasonable. Part of being unreasonable, you don't judge according to appearances. Part of being unreasonable, you can see it because you believe it. That's part of being unreasonable. You're like the Apostle Paul who said, "You must have the faith to call forth those things that be not as though they were." That's part of being unreasonable. Most people won't do that. Most people say, "Call me when you get it together then I'll support you."

Another empowering key to self-motivation is finding a cause larger than yourself. Find something that you can contribute to, somewhere you can make a difference. Part of what feeds your larger vision, part of what gives you a reason for being; part of what gives you your life is being able to give something back. You might hear, "I can't afford to give anything." But I say you can't afford not to give. Give your time. Give your talent. I don't know exactly what I'm going to do but I'm going over there. It's part of my tithing in the universe.

When you develop that special sense of mission when you're part of a cause larger than yourself, it drives you. You don't need an alarm clock to get up in the morning. You have special power. You'll go places and folks will like to be around you. They will know there's something different about you. They'll respond, "I want to know who you are. I just want to be near you." That energy that you have, that consciousness that you will embody will affect everybody around you.

Create a home-court advantage for yourself. You've got to be aware of who you have around you. You want to be selective. Have friends that will enable you to grow. I have friends that help me to grow spiritually. These are my spiritual friends. We talk about spiritual matters. I have other friends who are intellectual friends who help me grow intellectually and make me stretch. I have some professional friends. I'm a member of the National Speakers Association. I get together with other speakers and we learn from each other and we grow from each other.

Other people are social friends. We get together for the game or go out dancing or to the movies or to a restaurant. No serious, heavy, conversations here— they're not that kind of relationship. With other friends all we can do is walk together and talk about losing weight and being healthy. That's all we do. Nothing else. We grow from the people around us and the relationships and projects that we develop can enhance and can enrich our lives or they can drain us.

I know many talented people who had a great deal of potential but didn't surround themselves with other people who could inspire them to transcend themselves. Sadly they never realized their greatness, and they will end up going to their grave with all the good stuff still in them. You want to look at your relationships, the people who you're involved with, the people who you communicate with most often, and you want to ask yourself the question, "What am I becoming because of this relationship? Does it inspire me? Am I motivated? Am I encouraged? Am I driven to develop myself? Am I seeking my own greatness? What kind of person am I becoming because of this relationship? Am I becoming more cynical and negative about life?" Ask yourself that.

The next thing is that you've got to say yes to your life. You've got to say, "Yes, yes, to my dreams. Yes to me. Yes, I can make it. Yes, I can. Doesn't matter how many failures I've made. Doesn't matter how many mistakes I've endured. Doesn't matter about my defeats. Doesn't matter about what I've done. Yes. Yes. I don't care about the fact I'm in a hole now. Doesn't matter about where I am. Yes. The last chapter to my life has not been written yet. If you judge me now, you judge me prematurely. I haven't exposed all my stuff yet. I'm still in the process of transforming my life. I'm still in the process of becoming. Yes."

One time I had somebody in my life tell me, "You will never make it," and I said, "I'll show you." What energized me, what motivated me, was something that

Frank Sinatra said. He said, "The best revenge is massive success."

"I'll show you. You just watch my smoke," as old folks used to say. So, say yes. Stand up for your dreams. Stand up for what you want in your life. Decide that your life is so meaningful to you, that you love you and you love life so much that you're going to stand up for something you want.

I used to have a saying when I was on the radio, "Stand up for what you believe in because you can fall for anything."

Stand up for yourself and know that you are powerful. You have miracle-working power in your life right now, but you have to work on yourself. Develop yourself. Talk to yourself, day in and day out, selling yourself on you and on your potential. Know that you are worth all of your effort and that they key to your motivation as you get a larger vision of yourself, is to know that you have something to give, is to know that you have a reason for being in the universe at this point in time. I want you to stand up for your life right now. Stand up for your dream.

CHAPTER 16

The Power of Giving

Whatever you give, it's going to come back. It might not come back through that channel, but it's going to come back. Why? Because it is a universal law. We've all heard the saying, "As you sow, so shall you reap." We usually say that in a negative context but let's look at the positive side of that. That if you sow some good stuff out here, if you make it your business to give the best that you have, to give love, to give encouragement, to give help, to give support, I guarantee you, it's going to come back. If that's what your life is about, whatever you put out here, it's going to come back. The reason that most people don't give is because they operate out of a consciousness of scarcity. They don't believe that there's enough to go around. They can't see themselves having the capacity to give. They don't believe that they have anything to offer. They don't see themselves as an opening for the universe to work through, so if you begin to look at this new era that we're in, begin to see yourself as an opening for the universe to move through, to work through, to make a difference in life. See yourself being used by life to improve the quality of life, to expand, and to grow. Most people have a very limited view of themselves and a very limited view of the universe. They do not see their relationship to the universe, and cannot see how energy and things flow through them.

In *The Prophet*, Kahlil Gibran wrote, "A rich man speak to us of giving," and he answered, "You give but little when you give of your possessions, but it's when you give of yourself that you truly give." Gibran goes on to say that, "Those who give little of the much which they have, and they give it for recognition, and their hidden desire makes their gifts unwholesome," and we know people who give only to be recognized.

I love that old saying, "Judge a man not by what he does but by that which he doesn't have to do, and to judge the true quality of a man is what he'd do when nobody is looking."

Gibran says, "And there are those who have little and give it all." These are the believers in life and the bounty of life. Most people don't give because they don't believe in life. They don't understand the abundance in life, and so they go through life holding back—holding back on life—not understanding this also, that what you hold back from life, life holds back from you. Most of us go through life not giving. We're cheating ourselves, and also cheating life. I believe that all of us have some work to do. I strongly believe that each one of us showed up to do something, that each one of us showed up to contribute something to life, and that if we don't do it, it will not be done.

No one is going to give Les Brown's speech. No one is going to write your book. If you've been given something to do and you don't do it, you're short-circuiting the flow of the universe. Just imagine, if you please, people standing around a circle. We are given a bucket of love. I pass it to the person on my right, and they pass it to somebody on their right, and on and on, passing it until it comes back to me. One of the great things about giving is that as you give, you're going to receive. What we want to do is keep the flow going. If anybody gets the bucket of love and stops and holds it there, all of us suffer. They have short-circuited the flow that stopped what was going on, the energy that was going around. See, you are part of an equation and you are needed. Part of what I wish we'd all begin to look at is how we give up on our lives and that we've all got to begin to see what we're supposed to be doing?

We need to ask ourselves, "What is my life work?" and then give ourselves to that because as we do, we will be in a better position to take on this new era that we're in. If you decide to start living life generously—to start giving more of yourself, to start putting out more, contributing more to life—I guarantee you that life will take on a whole new meaning for you. As you begin to give more of yourself in your work, give more of yourself in your marriage, give more of yourself in your relationships with your families and friends, give more of yourself to your talents, vocation, job or business, life takes on a whole new dimension and you'll be happier.

As you begin to set higher standards for sharing your true self with the universe, you'll have a greater sense of fulfillment in life. Now, this does not mean no problems or challenges exist in your life. You will not be exempted from life's challenges but you will begin to see newer horizons. You will begin to see life differently from most people. I think when Henry David Thoreau said, "The mass of men lead lives of quiet desperation," he meant that we're going through life getting up in the morning for no reason because we're not using that which we have been given.

Once you discover your purpose in life and decide to live a life of sharing and contributing to life, you won't need an alarm clock to get up. You'll move differently. It will be easier to smile. Many folks appear listless, lifeless and find it hard to smile. Many are abusing themselves with alcohol and drugs, evading their own greatness and holding back on themselves. For years, I was cheating myself. For years, I could have been doing exactly what I'm doing right now, but I was afraid. I didn't feel I was worthy and I couldn't recognize that which I have been given. I had a limited view of me and I was literally running away from me. Life sometimes chases us and says, "No, no, no. We want you to do something great." We refuse. "No, not me. Go get somebody else. You're not talking about me. You don't know what I've been doing. No, no." But life knows. "Actually yes, we want you. We'll groom you and train you and get you ready." "Me?" "Yes. You," "Are you sure, me?" "Yes." "No. Not me. I don't want to do that." Then life just gets tired of chasing and sends you what my mother would call a whooping—shut up, straighten up and knock some sense into you. Then, after a while, you say, "Okay, okay, okay."

One of the reasons we should begin to give more is because we owe a debt. John Powell said, "I am afraid to tell you who I am, because, if I tell you who I am, you might not like who I am and that's all I have." He has another saying I love to quote, "We are made by those who love us and by those who refuse to love us."

When you are reading this book or perhaps hearing me speak, remember it's not just Les Brown talking to you. A lot of people have contributed to make me who I am right now. None of us are here because of our own doing. All of us have had life contribute to us.

We all have cookie people in our lives. What do I mean by cookie people? Cookie people and chicken soup people are people like Ms. Lillian. As a kid, I was always getting in trouble and my mother would whoop me. Ms. Lillian would hear me carrying on and afterwards would come over with cookies and milk. She'd say, "Here you are, Leslie. Even though you're a bad little boy, I brought you some cookies." Cookie people are those who look beyond your faults and see your needs. Even when you're behaving badly, even when you're not being who you really are, even if you're a moody person—these cookie people love you unconditionally. Chicken soup people are those you can call at 2:00 in the morning to say, "I got a flat tire. Will you come help me?" or "My battery is not running. Would you come give me a jump?" or "I need some help. Would you come get me out of jail?" If you don't have any chicken soup people in your life, I hope you can get some; we all need people we can count on for help. I'm encouraging you to write a letter of appreciation to the cookie people in your life before it's too late. Reach out to those who were a leg up for you, who contributed to you being who you are, and simply say, "I was just reminiscing over the years. You know I love you and appreciate everything you've been to me, and I just wanted to drop you this letter." How do you think they'd feel if they got that, out of nowhere? "Just want to thank you for how you have enriched my life. You might not have thought much of it but because of the help and assistance you gave me on that particular day, that was a turning point in my life."

Why should we give? Giving creates a vacuum and as we know, nature abhors a vacuum. So, when you give, you create a vacuum and now you are in a position to receive. If I have my arms closed holding on to everything I've got, nothing is available to come in. But if I'm open, I've created a vacuum thereby giving and keeping the flow going, the stuff in the universe is going to come back to me. It's going to come back, whatever you give. Whenever I go into a room and give a speech to inspire people to help them develop their greatness, I am also inspiring and challenging myself. As Richard Bach says, "We teach best what we most need to learn."

I'm not wearing any crown. I need it as much as I'm sharing it. I'm still growing, still unfolding, still seeking to discover my greatness. If you get ten percent of what I get as I walk out of here, you will be as different a person walking out as I am. The more I give to you, the more I get. Please understand that. It's a law of life. Do you know that we can literally eliminate poverty overnight? We could eliminate hunger and homelessness overnight if people understood the concept of what giving means, and the power in it—about the difference that it can make in our lives.

Go to any underserved neighborhood and interview the people there, evaluate their lifestyles and what they're doing, and what they're contributing to life. Then go to a wealthy neighborhood, and talk to those people, and evaluate them, and check out what they are doing with their energy and their time, and what they are contributing to life. You're going to discover, what Earl Nightingale said, "Our success in life is directly related to the quantity and the quality of the service that we give." You will find that people who have more, people that are living the abundant life are the contributors to life. They are the people that are giving more. The people who are operating out of scarcity and poverty consciousness are the people that are down and out. These are the people that are complaining and are blaming the world and everybody else for where they are. But if they took that same energy and begin to invest in themselves they would find their way towards giving something back to life and becoming a contributor.

I was in New Jersey to give a political presentation to a community group trying organize to revitalize their community. During a tour of a housing project my guide was proudly telling me, "This city is about to give $55 million to renovate these housing projects."

I said, "What a waste." Surprised, the guide asked me why I would say that. I turned and asked the person who we had just met on the tour if he lived in this building. He said he did, so I asked how many families lived here. He answered, "Six families."

I said, "When we walked in the door just now we smelled the stench of urine right away. It doesn't take a genius to go down to the store and perhaps sacrifice buying three packs of cigarettes, and buy some type of soap and water, and come back here and wash this stench out of here. It doesn't take a genius to get a can of paint and paint over the graffiti, and repair the mailbox. I say if you pour that money into these housing projects and you don't first change the people who are living here, this will be right back to where it was before."

I know there are many situations where people need some help and assistance, but people must be allowed to contribute. I say they should pay for the paint and for the mailboxes and broken windows to be repaired. And I guarantee if the children are outside throwing a ball they'll be saying, "Don't you dare hit that window. Do you know how much I paid for that window?" It makes a difference. People need to be given the opportunity to take responsibility, to contribute and invest in life, and then life is appreciated. We don't want to just give blindly. You want to give to people who are out there struggling and trying to make an impact in the universe. I'd rather give to a man who's already doing it than somebody over here doing nothing and complaining. Man, why don't you get up and do something? I think if you have to go over there and get them up, you'll have to do that for the rest of your life, so do it with those who are already doing it.

You want to keep the flow going by working with people who are contributors to life. There's a scripture I couldn't understand when I first heard it and I thought it was very cold. "For he that hath, to him shall be given and he shall have more abundance; but whosoever hath not, from him shall be taken even that which he hath." At first I thought, "Now, that's not fair." But now that I understand it I see it is completely fair. "He that hath" is the key. Those that have a generous view of life, those that have courage and initiative, and those that have resourcefulness shall get. Don't be like the bellman in my hotel who, when I said, "I need to get my shoes shined," said, "I don't shine shoes." I asked him how long he had been working there. He said about three months. Then I asked him what he was doing before then. He said, "I just got out of the joint." So, he won't shine shoes. That's beneath him, but it was okay to steal. That wasn't beneath him? Beware the taker, the complainer and the blamer and look for the contributors, the growers and the doers.

Here's something else you're going to discover in giving. It is very important to give thanks. Giving thanks creates power. Give thanks for your house. Give thanks for your apartment, your car, your family, for your health, your relationships, for what you have. When we focus on something, it expands. Whatever you focus on, that's what you're going to continue to multiply and expand in your life. But if you focus on what you don't have, if all you can do is point out the negative things in your life, whatever you focus on, you're going to expand that.

Some people, all they can do is complain. They can't find anything good to say about life and about anybody else. Every time they open their mouths, that's what their minds are consumed with, and that's all they're producing in their lives. These are people that you don't want to be around. Develop a spirit of gratitude. I'm thankful for life. I'm thankful to be an American. I'm thankful to be on this part of the planet. I'm thankful to see another day. I don't have all the things I want to have, but I'm thankful that I'm still here. I have another opportunity, another day to live, another chance to contribute, another chance to make a difference in life. Begin to give thanks for what you have. Whatever you focus on, remember now, you want to become aligned with the universe. If you have scarcity in your life, it's because you have a consciousness of scarcity. Become thankful for what you have, for the abundance that you're attracting, for the good relationships coming your way right now. Become thankful as this will help you to create incredible opportunities and will help you improve your life and the quality of life of the people around you.

Learning to give also means learning to give forgiveness. Many of us do not realize we are blocking ourselves, we are blocking our good in the universe, and we're literally standing in the way of the flow of what life has for us because we haven't learned how to forgive. We haven't learned how to let things go so we can get on with our lives. When we forgive, it's not for the other person. It's not because they deserved or earned it. It's for us, it's for you. Most importantly, you've got to forgive yourself first, and learn how to let that baggage go. As Paul said to the Philippians, "Forgetting those things which are behind, reaching forward to those things which are ahead."

Let's consider how giving empowers you and makes you powerful in the world. The more you give to life, the more you're able to get from life. Many of us go through life feeling that we don't have enough to share, feeling that we will be depleted if we give of our resources. We don't see ourselves connected to the abundance of life. I feel very strongly that we can make an incredible difference in life. Phyllis Marks said, "Giving empowers you because taken to its ultimate, what you are really giving is love. Love is the motivating force behind the infinite supply of universal energy. Love truly makes the world go round and as with anything circular, it's going to keep coming back." Phyllis is right, so as she continues to give love and hope to these people, she receives love and hope for herself, and helping to begin to restructure and redesign the kind of life that she wants.

We all have had experiences in our lives that will weigh us down if we allow it. If we allow it we could carry this baggage through our lives, letting it hold us down, stifling our potential to give and to contribute in life. If we continue to carry all that baggage, we can never be open to the love, abundance and opportunity life has to offer us because we are so full with all that baggage.

This story of the monkey trap illustrates how holding onto baggage can get in our way. This is a story, a parable, and could be a real way of trapping monkeys. The trap is to put nuts or rice or other food inside of a bottle or jar or even a hole in the ground. The monkeys are curious and hungry and reach inside. Then they are unable pull their hand out because the hole is not big enough for their clenched fist to pass back out and they won't let go of their fistful of treats. Unable to remove their hand, they are easily captured. All they had to do was to let the nuts go. A lot of us act like this with our own baggage, we just keep holding on like we're crazy. Let go and run and be free.

Let's look at more ways giving creates energy in ourselves and in others. Have you ever helped a blind or elderly person across the street, or offered help to anyone during your day? Just simple acts like holding a door or the elevator gives us a good feeling inside. That good feeling creates good energy which we're giving to that person out in the world, but we're really giving to ourselves. That's really the law—when you are giving *of* yourself, you are giving *to* yourself.

In his book, *Critique of Pure Reasoning*, Immanuel Kant said, "Sometimes, we must give out of a sense of oughtness, that certain things happen that we just say something ought to be done about this."

A policeman in Washington, D.C. was on patrol, and he came upon a car in a park, and the car was running. He saw a figure slumped over the steering wheel and discovered a fourteen-year-old boy with a bullet through the back of his head. That could have been his son. He said, "Something ought to be done. We're losing too many young people."

He had several thousand dollars' worth of exercise equipment in his basement. He rented a place. He started bringing kids in to get them involved in taking care of their bodies with physical exercise and athletic activity. He then expanded to getting them involved in entrepreneurial ventures, saying that this is a free enterprise system, and the more enterprising you are, the freer you are. Now these kids have started their own business. They have a little shopping center that they operate and manage; they even have commercials on the radio to promote their business. All this because that cop said "I ought to do something."

He could have said, "It's just no use. It's out of control now." We all can have that inner voice telling us that it's a waste of our time, energy and effort. I say don't listen to it. Be like the DC policeman and choose to listen to that other small voice that says, "I can do something and I ought to do it."

Benjamin Disraeli said, "A human being with a settled purpose must accomplish it, and nothing can resist a will which will stake even existence upon its fulfillment." I strongly believe that if we get up in the morning each day out of a sense of oughtness and decide that "I am an opening for the universe, that life can work through and use me as a channel and as an instrument for change," we can make a difference in those areas that we're concerned about.

How are we going to do it? We don't know, but we know that we can make a difference. We might not be here to see the results of our efforts. I like to focus on the second verse of *Lift Every Voice and Sing* by civil rights activist and poet James Weldon Johnson:

Stony the road we trod,
Bitter the chastening rod,
Felt in the days when hope unborn had died;
Yet with a steady beat,
Have not our weary feet
Come to the place for which our fathers sighed?
We have come over a way that with tears has been
*   watered,*
We have come, treading our path through the blood of
*   the slaughtered,*
Out from the gloomy past,
Till now we stand at last
Where the white beam of our bright star is cast.

Somebody paid the price for us to be here and as we begin to look toward the future, we all have an obligation to give something back. A lot of us don't give more because we allow ego to get in the way.

A well-dressed man was walking through a neighborhood one day. A woman came to the door and said, "Hey, you." He stopped and said very politely, "Yes, ma'am?" She said, "Come here." He came to her, "Yes? What may I do for you, ma'am?" She said, "I want you to cut my wood." He said, "Yes, ma'am." He removed his coat, took the ax and cut the wood. She said, "Won't you take some around the back and put some in the fireplace?" He said, "Yes, ma'am," and he did just that.

After he finished, she said, "What do I owe you?" He said, "Nothing ma'am. Thank you for the opportunity to serve you." She said, "Okay." He left, walking down the street with his coat over his shoulder. Her maid came up asking, "Do you know who that was?" The woman she worked for said she did not. The maid replied, "That's the great Negro educator, Booker T. Washington." She looked out the window and said, "Is that right?" Then said, "Send for him," and that woman, who Booker T. Washington cut the wood for, contributed several million dollars to his dream of building an institution of higher learning, Tuskegee Institute, that is still standing today.

What if he had said, "Do what? Cut your wood? Don't even come up in here with that kind of stuff. You better cut your own wood if you want to get it cut." He didn't allow his ego to get in the way. He gave what he had. He contributed. How much have we denied ourselves? How much have we blocked ourselves because we allowed that little ego to get in the way, to prevent us from giving and serving which is the essence of life? It's about service. I say as you look out on the future, decide that you are going to allow your life to be a life of service. Decide that you are going to give more than you have ever given before. Decide that each day that you are given life, that you're going to make a difference with your life, that you're going to make a statement with your life, that once again, as opposed to sitting by, feeling like a victim, that you're going to see yourself as a channel, as an opening for the universe to work through, and that you'll say to life, "Use me. Oh, use me. I've got more to give, use me."

Here is an affirmation to read often and say out loud:

I want life to use me.

I want to give more,

Share more,

Be an expression of love,

Be an instrument of hope,

To impact our youth,

To re-create their future.

I'm grateful for life.

I'm grateful for being here.

I'm grateful to be able to serve.

I'm grateful.

CHAPTER 17

The Power of Perseverance

For this final chapter let's look at overcoming insurmountable odds when things seem bigger than what you can handle. It's one thing to get out of a $5 jam. It's another thing to get out of a $5,000 jam or a $50,000 jam. It's one thing to have a headache and know you can take an aspirin. It's another thing to have a doctor give you a report that what you have is "incurable." We want to look at what you do when things seem bigger than you are, when you don't know any natural way out of the situation. As an example, let's look at something everybody's familiar with—money. What happens when you need $1,200 by next week and you have no natural way of getting that money? What do you do?

There certainly are times when we feel like that, when we say, "I don't have any idea whatsoever of how I'm going to pull this out." I've been in situations like that where I had deadlines I didn't meet, I lost a car, lost a home, power was turned off, and telephone cut off. Things like this are going to happen to us at different points in life. What does it mean? It really doesn't mean anything. It's not important at all. It's just a temporary inconvenience because all of those things can be corrected. It's a part of the process that we all go through.

The challenge, in the midst of all of these things, is to stay focused on your goal, and to maintain your expectations of making it happen—keeping your energy positive and relentlessly looking for ways in which to pull it out. I guarantee you that there will be some intervention. What causes it? I don't know. It can seem supernatural. Here's an example from my life.

I remember the exact date I lost my job after being fired from broadcasting, September 18th, 1978. I was behind in my mortgage payments and my house was up for foreclosure. I had done everything I could. I had borrowed as much money as I could borrow. I talked to family members and friends. I was unemployed for several months, applying for job after job, yet nothing was happening. I couldn't get enough money to save the house, but I never felt that I was actually going to lose that house. This is very important, the feeling that I had. I wanted that house.

What I did next was very uncanny. I released it. I knew that I had done the best that I could. At that time, with the limited money that I did have, I decided to take a trip with my family to Miami, to spend time in the sun with my wife and children. We caught a Greyhound bus from Columbus, Ohio to Florida. We arrived on the day that the bank was to foreclose on the house at 12:00 p.m. when I got a call from my former assistant who had gone by the house. "Les, it's an emergency, call Columbus right away." I did and she said, "Les, you won't believe this. You have a check from the Internal Revenue Service, it's your income tax refund, and it's enough to pay the house notes." And I had money left over! I never received a refund prior to that time nor since, and I did not lose the house.

There are things that we don't understand but we have seen that if we act in certain ways, things begin to happen that are in our favor, things that show us that the universe is on our side. I believe that if we begin to align our thoughts with action, if we are relentless and focused, then we will find everything we're seeking. If necessary we may have to try one hundred things, or five hundred things, or ten thousand things as Edison did, until we find a way out.

Sometimes we eliminate possibilities for ourselves because we really don't do all we can. I think A.L. Williams was spot on with the title of his book, *All You Can Do Is All You Can Do But All You Can Do Is Enough.*

I think that my commitment is stronger than most people's but if I had to literally measure my commitment I might have given about eighteen to twenty percent of what I'm really capable of. Compared with where I used to be, I believe I am getting to higher levels of consciousness, yet I'm still nowhere near reaching fifty percent of the commitment that I can make to accelerate the growth and development of my dreams and the manifestation of the things that I know within myself that I'm capable of producing.

Our biggest challenge is beginning to look within ourselves to remove those energy blocks. If we are not producing the income that we want, let us not to look outside of ourselves but look within ourselves and ask some questions. How am I blocking myself? Am I really giving it all that I have? Am I really being as creative as I can be? Am I really unstoppable? Am I as relentless as I can be? Am I exhausting every means possible? Am I turning up every rock to find what it is that I'm looking for? What resides between our ears when we're examining how to come up with $500, $1,200, or $2,000 is the same gray matter that resides between the ears of a Ross Perot or a JP Morgan. How is it that one man or woman can do it and repeat it again and again, and that so many others just can't? It has to be consciousness. When we talk about consciousness, we're talking about a collection of our thoughts, our feelings, our emotions and experiences, all used as an active force to produce in our lives, that which we want to produce. Everything that exists in life—from the shoes on our feet, the chairs we're sitting in, the clothes we're wearing, the homes we live in, the cars we drive—all came out of our consciousness, from the invisible into the visible. Man was a vehicle, the outlet to produce that.

What happens when a person is pursuing their dream and they get stuck—saying I tried it, but it didn't work? Apparently, something stopped them in midstream. Perhaps it was something that they felt they couldn't surmount? It seemed as though they were stuck and there was no way out, so they gave up and said it didn't work. Anybody that has fallen short of their goals ran into something that they were not willing to handle. In order to reach your dream, in order to make things happen, there must be a willingness to do what is required. Let's say the need is to raise $2,000 and like me you have a set of recordings you can sell for $40. Are you willing to make 200 calls a day? Are you willing to stand on a corner, talk to people and say, "Listen, I've got a set of recordings here that can change your life?"

Are you willing to make the commitment that you will not go to sleep until you sell at least ten a day? Are you willing to say, "I'll do it if it takes me twelve hours walking and talking to people until I find ten people to say yes?" If I have to talk to 200 people or 300 people in order to provide food for my family, to provide shelter, to not to have creditors hounding me, am I willing to do that? Am I willing to stand in an airport and sell them? Am I willing to go out and make calls again and again and again? Am I willing to knock on doors? Am I willing?

If we have some skill, ability, knowledge, or product, then the only thing that's between us and what we want to generate is our willingness to expend the energy to produce the results that we want. Am I willing to wash cars? Am I willing to scrub floors? Am I willing to wash dishes? Am I willing to go out and speak or do seminars or workshops? What am I willing to do with my energy, my time and my knowledge to produce the results? That's the bottom line. What are you willing to do? Many people don't give up on their goals because it becomes insurmountable or impossible. Too often they looked at what they wanted and just decided within themselves consciously or unconsciously, "I'm not willing to produce this result." So, ask yourself if you are you willing to say, "I need $2,000 between now and next week and come hell or high water, I will produce that?" That's the bottom line. The only thing that counts in life are results, not reasons explaining why you didn't do it. We are capable of producing results. Are you willing to honor your commitment to do that? What are you willing to do? How many floors are you willing to mop? How many shoes are you willing to shine? How many phone calls are you willing to make? How many sales calls are you willing to make? How many jobs are you willing to hold? How much service are you willing to provide?

Many times, people don't keep their commitments. They are not willing to be a no-matter-what person, the kind of person that says, "I'm going to make this happen no matter what." Many use escape routes for themselves or point to some reason for not producing results. People weren't buying or the economy is soft. Somebody somewhere is buying. Somebody somewhere is spending some money.

When I was working on developing my dream I started thinking, "If Walt Disney can do it, if John D. Rockefeller can do it, then I can do it." Am I to believe that they have some license of exclusivity on producing wealth or results that I don't have? In his book, *Succeeding Against the Odds,* John H. Johnson said, "For it is the most enduring element of our faith that I must conclude this speech by saying that men and women are limited not by the place of their birth, not by the color of their skin but by the size of their hope." What is the size of your hope? As we begin to look at what it is we want to produce in our lives, I think another question to ask ourselves is, "What is the size of our commitment to make it happen?"

When you ask people to become a no-matter-what person, something inside of them begins to tremble because of the fact that we aren't accustomed to saying, "I'm going to make this happen." Most people won't do that, they won't take that kind of stand, saying, "I'm going to make this happen no matter what." It takes energy, conviction, determination and a mindset to say, "I'm going to do this."

Goethe said, "Once you make a commitment, providence moves too. All kinds of things happen that never would have happened." I know from my own life that a whole stream of things can happen that you could never anticipate. I know that.

I think that Longfellow was right when he said, "If you go to the gate and you knock loud enough and long enough, somebody is going to answer." It's the same thing with anything in life. If you knock long enough and hard enough, somebody is going to answer. We might think, "Suppose they don't answer?" I say to you, they will. This is all about your own personal power. Know that it is your understanding and commitment that open the doors for you. Many people are victims of the personal power of others but have never activated their own personal power.

What about those instances in which we have failed? One of the valuable things I have learned how to do is to detach myself, to not buy into it. I have learned to view disappointments and setbacks according to appearances only. I see them as little projects to be worked out, a challenge to my wits, saying, "Hey, how much do you really want it? How creative are you? How resourceful are you? How unstoppable are you? How determined are you? How bad do you want it? How hungry are you?" I see life waltzing with me, saying, "You want to Tango? Come on. You want this? You're willing to run over here? Come on. Are you willing to climb this mountain here? Come on. Are you willing to hold your breath and try and swim down to this level? Come on." I see it as a challenge that introduces me to myself. We all have to look at life like that. I think it's a little game.

Start to embrace only those things that are for our highest good. No one has the right to determine or has the knowledge to say how long we're going to be here. We can choose to surrender or we can choose to take a stand and fight. There are a lot of people who fight who are still here. There are people who fight and who go. At least they go out fighting. They didn't just surrender. They didn't just throw in the towel on themselves.

What I'm saying is that there is something in us. There's a power and an energy that's in us that we owe to ourselves to take on anything. Disease in the body, poverty, opposition, whatever is between us and that which we desire and feel will give us a rich and full life—we should fight for it. You've just got to decide that your life is worth this kind of effort and fight with everything in you night and day with every breath that you have.

Many people don't have that kind of fighting spirit. Many people expend more energy watching a football game, a basketball game, or some type of sporting event than they will give to their dream. They have spent more time talking about what happened on television, in some soap opera, or about some spectacular entertainment or stress-relieving activity than focusing on the possibilities for their own lives. They don't get that excited about themselves and their own potential for greatness. I'm saying that we need to start focusing on ourselves and using our energies to move us from where we are into the direction of where we want to go, overcoming the automatic mind.

As we work on ourselves constantly, we will find that we become in alignment with the universe and we are able to produce what appear to be miracles to most people but are really a perfect demonstration of the law of working in harmony with the universe. The key to it is having a whole vision of what you want to create, of constantly working with your feelings and your energy, of keeping it positive, of engaging in actions and having things, friends, relationships, goals and scriptures that challenge you and help create this new reality for yourself. As you continue to hold that vision in focus, as you continue to charge it with words and to act as if it already is, when you finally hit that level of consciousness, it will manifest.

People come out of nowhere and support you. You get unexpected money that you had no idea was going to come your way. Help and assistance from strangers will come to you and you'll say, "Whoa." You begin to discover things showing up that you need that you didn't even know you needed. And they are right here at your disposal when you get to that new level of consciousness.

The key is dogged determination, which I've observed and learned from the people who I have read, including Thomas Edison, all the great inventors, John H. Johnson, Dr. Norman Vincent Peale, George Washington Carver, and Dr. Benjamin Mays to name just a few. They all had dogged determination. They knew it, they saw it, they felt it, and they experienced it. There was a consciousness about them. I think the greatest manifestation of this in our time is Nelson Mandela. So many people who took the stand he took died, and he didn't. Why is that? What is it that will give a man or a woman that kind of determination to give up twenty-seven years of their lives, facing death every day, and not collapse, fall or surrender?

What is it about a human being? The human spirit is so enormously powerful beyond our wildest imagination that one entity could bring a political system to its knees or begin to dismantle an unjust form of government. What is it about a human being, about a Mother Teresa, about a Mahatma Gandhi, about a Benjamin Disraeli, about a Winston Churchill, about a Martin Luther King? What is it about those people that can affect humanity in such a way that changes history? I believe that whatever it is in them, we are all endowed with that as well. We have the capacity to produce those kinds of results in our own lives. We have the ability to align ourselves with something that will outlast us, something that is bigger than ourselves that will energize us and propel us to new levels of consciousness.

I don't *believe* these things work, I *know* they work. That's the only way that I've been able to achieve any success and to live my life. I am reminded that I must put these habits and knowledge to use every day. It is a breakthrough when you tap into the knowledge that you are involved in creating reality. The kind of person you must be in order to produce those results—the kind of thinking and the level of energy required—means that you are getting out of step with common thinking. You're marching to the beat of a different drummer. This can feel awkward and be lonely and strange, but it's okay.

The kind of person you become will give you a feeling of self-appreciation and self-respect. You'll be glad that life did not deny you the opportunity of experiencing all of what it has to offer.

Get to know yourself. Know that regardless of what's going on now, you are lovable, you are valuable, and you are a worthwhile person. You've been endowed with greatness. You have basic goodness which is the foundation for the greatness that you can ultimately achieve. You have a spiritual and moral obligation to do something with your life. You have a reason for being.

This is Mrs. Mamie Brown's baby boy, Leslie Calvin Brown, saying it's been a plum pleasing pleasure as well as a privilege to serve you. Thank you all for reading.